ANATOMY

OF

SUCCESS

*The Science of Inheriting
Your Brain's Wealth & Power
While You're Still Alive!*

ANATOMY

OF

SUCCESS

The Science of Inheriting
Your Brain's Wealth & Power
While You're Still Alive!

SALEEM
BIDAOUI

New York

Anatomy of Success
The Science of Inheriting Your Brain's Wealth & Power While You're Still Alive!

ISBN 978-1-60037-647-4

Library of Congress Control Number: 2009929138

MORGAN · JAMES
THE ENTREPRENEURIAL PUBLISHER

Morgan James Publishing, LLC
1225 Franklin Ave., STE 325
Garden City, NY 11530-1693
Toll Free 800-485-4943
www.MorganJamesPublishing.com

 In an effort to support local communities, raise awareness and funds, Morgan James Publishing donates one percent of all book sales for the life of each book to Habitat for Humanity. Get involved today, visit **www.HelpHabitatForHumanity.org**.

To the best part of me,
my loving wife Alia

TABLE OF CONTENTS

"When you suspect you're going wrong,
Or lack the strength to move along
With placid poise among your peers,
Because of haunting doubts or fears:
It's time for you to shift your pack,
And steer upon another tack!

When wind and waves assail your ship,
And anchors from the bottom slip;
When clouds of mist obscure your sun,
And foaming water madly run:
It's time for you to change your plan
And make a port while yet you can!

When men laugh at your woeful plight,
And seek your old repute to blight;
When all the world bestows a frown,
While you are sliding swiftly down:
It's time for you to show your grit.
And let the scoffers know you're fit!

When Failure opens your luckless door,
And struts across the creaking floor;
When Fortune flees and leaves you bare,
And former friends but coldly stare:
It's time for you to take a tack,
And show the world you're coming back!"

–Lilburn Harwood Townsend

Preface

———

Why is it that even though we are exposed to the same environment, opportunities, and abundance, some of us become millionaires while others barely make it through life? Does life "pick & choose" what we become or do we create our own lives as well as our destinies? Is the problem of not achieving what we want in life mainly "external" or is it "internal"?

Hello! My name is Saleem Bidaoui and I would like to congratulate you on purchasing and reading this invaluable book. What you are about to venture upon will elaborate on the questions above, shed light on why we only earn what *we* ask for in life, and how we may achieve favourable and long lasting results. Further, I will lay down not only the "ingredients" of success, but also the "recipe" to a happy and fulfilling life.

Now let me take a wild guess! Some of the questions that you may have asked yourself when you picked up this book were the following:

1. *Who is Saleem Bidaoui?*

2. *Is this book any different from other self-help books?*

3. *Will this book leave a real and long-lasting impression on me?*

I will tell you about myself in a minute and get ready for a shock when you read "My Story" right at the beginning of Part I. Before I do that, however, let me tell you a few words about *what this book will not do for you* because I think it is as important as what it may do for you.

This book will not change your life and no other book on earth can do so until you are sincerely willing and committed to achieving such a goal. A book that promises you a life change is mis-leading. Books and programmes can only provide you with the means to improve your life. They will not change your life. You do!

Those who promise you a life makeover in a month or less may label my words as "un-commercial". With respect to everybody's opinion though, what matters in here is you the reader and the beneficiary of the subject matter. It is of utmost importance to understand that anything you want to have, or be, in life must manifest within you first. All else is merely a medium. The best self-improvement tool ever invented cannot help you unless you are aware of it, believe that it can do so, you are willing to use it, and most importantly to keep on using it until you get what you want. This is the point I present in this book.

Moreover, this book is not a magic pill. If you are looking for one, just let me give you another reality check: *they haven't invented such a pill yet and never will!*

Therefore, my first and most crucial advice at the beginning of this book is to stop looking for the promise of happiness, success, and better life outside of yourself because my years of experience in this field says you will never find it as your first option. I've spent two decades searching for success and happiness without being aware that I already have them within me and until I acknowledged that fact I was just searching for a mirage. Mind you, I am not trying to spoil your dream, but instead, want to provide you with one that you can truly transform into reality. If that's what you really want, then you have a powerful tool and you are looking at it right now. Did my words wake you up somehow? Well, keep on reading and I promise you more surprises. Before I do that however, let me guess who you are first!

By choosing to read this book I think you belong to one of three categories. You are either:

I. A successful person who wants to add more fuel to his/her success.
II. <u>On</u> your way to success and need a catalyst to get you there faster and sooner. Or,
III. <u>In</u> the way of your own success and need all the tools you can get your hands on to change the status quo.

If you belong to one of the first two categories, then you just found a medium that will show you how to transform yourself, fine-tune your approach to life, and build or expand your success to any height you may desire. Nevertheless, it will draw to your attention things that have a tremendous impact on your life but you may have overlooked in the past.

If you belong to the third category, however, this book is definitely for you. I am sure you will agree with me that sometimes the experience we accumulate from failure is more rich and empowering than the one we acquire from success itself. Sometimes nothing brings us to the threshold of rebound faster than failure itself. Not surprisingly, most successful people you hear about today have been in the same category you maybe in right now and I was no different. Bear in mind that this is the main reason I wanted this book to be available to you.

By reading this introduction you may have a rough idea about my past. But so far you have no clue why and how I transformed myself to become a totally different person. So before we dive into the ingredients of success, how you can elevate yourself to a higher level in the game of life, and how you may get every cell in your body to help you achieve whatever you want in life, let me share with you a synopsis of my past life.

Part One.

THE INGREDIENTS

My Story

To conjure up the big picture, I find it imperative to start with a brief summary about my background and then quickly move to the events that changed my entire life and led to writing this book.

I grew up in a middle class, middle size family, and attended a relatively good school by my country's standards. At the age of seventeen I decided to drop out of school. My father wanted me to acquire a trade to secure my future and as such I started my career as an auto-body repairperson. Five to six years later my father retired from the car repair business and made up his mind to establish a home furnishing business instead. I joined him as an active partner and that business quickly became my ultimate goal and obsession in life. Giving it all we could, it sustained prosperity and expansion in no time. Three years later that business and my own apartment were reduced to rubble thanks to the cyclical wars in my country.

Frustrated with the calamity I went through I decided to immigrate to Canada. I arrived in my new homeland in 1982 and up until 1987 everything was fine. Then, and for many reasons that I find no need to mention in here, my life took a downward spiral and I went through chronic failure that dragged on for a while and then evolved to what I call a "3D" status. Do you know what the 3Ds of failure are? Well, it could be different things to different

3

people. In my case, it was debt, divorce, and depression. The worst you can ever experience, especially when combined, wrapped, and handed to you in one package.

After a while though, I thought I hit rock bottom and it was time to pick up the pieces and move on with my life but there was more, much more than I anticipated. As you can imagine, I had minimal education, every second word was a swear, I smoked like a chimney, and unlike today, I used to know it all. Do you get the picture of what kind of person I was? If you do not, just think of someone who's living in his or her own bubble and needs no one's advice on what to do with his/her life. Imprudent and naïve by choice is the least I can say about that era of my life. Yes, I do find it hard to admit. But that was my past and my past is something I cannot delete or change. The only thing I can do about it is to learn from those mistakes, improve my present, and use it to educate my kids and other people about the perils of such a destructive and irresponsible lifestyle.

To keep the story short, in 1990 I matured a bit, re-married, and in an attempt to change my luck, so to speak, my wife and I decided to move from Ottawa to Toronto. One year later things neither changed nor improved and we remained struggling. As a result, I was totally lost, confused, dejected, and drifting in life with no clear aim to where I was going. Any way was my way at the time!

As fate may have it, one day I was walking in the neighbourhood contemplating the best course of action I could take to get myself out of this mess, my eyes caught a billboard for a community college that read, "Admission test June 24th". I looked at it and said to myself, "What do I have to lose? Maybe a higher education is what I need to get my life back on track". Keep in mind that during that period I was unemployed, stressed out, and desperate for a change. Thus, without any hesitation I went into the admissions office, paid the fees, and then I went back a couple of weeks later and wrote the test.

Now, based on my qualifications, I was almost certain that I would not be accepted. Well, I was gladly wrong that time and the college welcomed me as a student. Now think about it. I dropped out of school in 1972 and then went back to school in 1992. Twenty years later, that is. So what am I trying to convey to you in this book?

The best lesson I've learned from that experience was the following:

It's never too late to go after what you want in life!

Here's a quote by English Philosopher George Eliot posted at the entrance of the University of Berkley in California:

"It is never too late to be what you might have been"

Frankly, it was quite challenging for me to attend college, especially after all of those years. I never finished high school to begin with. Just to give you an idea how tough it was in the first semester, while it took any regular student 2-3 hours to grasp a chapter it took me between 5-10 hours sometimes to absorb one chapter. That is how challenging it was for me in the beginning but with perseverance, enthusiasm, and high hopes things got easier. After I graduated from college there were no fireworks, and that's what makes life funny sometimes because misfortunes could be a blessing in disguise but we do not see it at the time.

In desperation, one day I went to my wife and said, "Honey, now I have a Business Administration Diploma under my belt and I am sick and tired of doing the odd jobs here and there. Why don't we go back home? We might have a better chance there!" Sure enough in 1997 we packed our suitcases and went back home. Luckily, two months later I landed a job that changed the entire course of my life. Unfortunately though, that job did not last for too long for all of the obvious reasons I mentioned earlier. Nevertheless, I sustained the status quo up until the year 1999. It was then for the first time I realized that there was something wrong with my approach to life and not the other way around.

I realized that by and large the world only reflects back our own attitude. If you ask me about my attitude prior to that awakening, one of things I can mention is that I used to snap like a cobra, and for trivial reasons. I used to think that no one wants to help me succeed because people are nasty, selfish, and the whole world was conspiring against me. Unfortunately, all of these were realities that only existed in my mind. They were realities of my own making, that is. Realities I insisted on seeing due to the circumstances I was going through at the time.

With my paradigm shift, however, I asked myself, "How could anyone succeed with this kind of attitude?" It was a shift that triggered a 180 degrees transformation within me. I felt I was born again with a new philosophy, attitude, and perspective on life.

I simply changed the way I *think* and everything in my life changed to the way I *think*.

You can say that again!

That change propelled me to search for the major causes of success, and failure, as it was in my case. I became obsessed with "Why did all of that happen to me, and how can anyone transform and turn his/her life around?"

I ventured for insights about the subject and it took me a bit over five years of extensive research to reach what I am going to share with you in this book. Does it mean that now I know it all? Honestly, far from it! It is just that I had the opportunity to go through a lot of books, CDs, and seminars, and all I did after was merely attempt to link the dots. Does it mean that I wrote this book just for people who failed and keep on failing? Well, one aspect of the book is to show you how to avoid failure. The other, however, is about how to achieve genuine success and reap the rewards that comes with it, regardless of where you are on the stage of life.

As I started probing I discovered that some of the "How To Get Rich" books and seminars could cause more damage than repair by inadvertently inducing further self-doubt in people who are not ready for them yet. Do not get me wrong. I am not judging the value or impact of any program in the market today and I am not saying that such books are useless. It is just that I classify some of these books and seminars as step #2, where step #1 remains a prerequisite to our success and in some cases still missing. If so, then what is step #1, you might ask?

The most important key to your success, happiness, and better life, is to know your-self, *first*.

This is the ultimate secret that's been overlooked by the majority of health, wealth, and happiness seekers.

Each year millions of people in North America alone attend *"How to become a millionaire"* seminars, yet only a fraction of those who attend make it to the greener side within the first five years. If that is the case, then why do a good number of those participants not become wealthy in spite of the abundance and the means available to them to achieve such a goal? Do they, or don't they, want to get rich? I am sure you will agree with me that every human being on earth loves to become wealthy, with the exception of a few monks, of course. This love of wealth is engrained in our genes as we shall see.

Unfortunately, some people seek success and wealth externally long before they internally get themselves ready for it. As such, they do not, and will not, achieve it. For such people, even if they coincidently stumble on it they will lose it faster than when they first accumulated it. Examples of those are many, and I will tell you why as we move along.

It is imperative to understand, however, that success and wealth are universal and up for grabs by anyone and anywhere except in the minds of unsuccessful people. Do not take my word for it, just look around you. In fact, I know of no country that has no successful and no wealthy people within its borders. Nonetheless, I know of no country that doesn't have those whom *voluntarily* deprive themselves from success.

Externally therefore, success is out there waiting to offer its status to anyone who's willing to earn it. Success is unbiased and doesn't really care who you are or where you came from. Just meet its criteria and it will accept you as a member. Internally though, unless you align yourself with it first, you will neither experience it, nor achieve such a status. That is to say, when you are not internally ready for it, externally it will not "click". Most people in this world passively try to succeed and when success doesn't come easily, they automatically settle for an inferior opportunity. Some start with an ambition of a doctor, for example, and then it becomes okay to be a nurse. That's exactly how I messed up my life, by the way!

In the next nine chapters we will talk about the genetic roots of success, how to distinguish between the *"Hardware"* and *"Software"* of your biological structure, and how to get your mind, body, heart, and soul in synch because this is the only way to align yourself with the kind of life that you really want and deserve. Let me warn you though! Some of the things you will read about might seem somewhat mundane in the beginning. However, I find it necessary for you to see the details of your life's portrait before examining the portrait as a whole. Just bear in mind that I am not trying to tell you things just to impress you, but to guide you through a journey like no other. It is a journey to self-discovery.

What you are about to read and indulge yourself in is simply *"The Science of Neuro-Success"* and a journey that depicts the molecular structure of success and how to achieve it *permanently*. Having said that, here is my promise to you:

By the time you finish reading this book your life will never be the same.

I strongly recommend that you read this book more than once. Any time you find yourself faced with a new concept and still cannot see the big picture behind that concept, please go back and read it again. Don't worry if something doesn't click the first time you read it because I will be linking everything together and you'll see the big picture as we move along.

In the first part of the book I will tell you about why things may, or may never, happen in your life, regardless of what you might wish or do. In the second part I will provide you with what I call *"Your Success Recipe"*. When you integrate this recipe and apply all of its ingredients you'll feel the change in every aspect of your life, and in no time. You might be wondering about my definition of success as well as about what I mean by *"Permanent Success"*.

Here is my definition to both:

- "Success is the *realization* of something you love to be or do for the rest of your life"
- "Permanent Success is the *conviction* that you can get there"

Does it mean that by following the recipe laid out in this book you will never fail? Although I wish I could say that, this will never be the case. Ironically, no one wants to fail yet no one is immune to it and as paradoxical as it may seem, you need your failures in order for you to succeed and I will explain that later on. Permanent success does not mean that you will never fail. It simply means that you will look at and deal with every failure as a stepping-stone to your long-term success. It also means that no matter how many times life challenges you; you strongly believe that you can handle it and will succeed.

Chapter 1

You Are Born
To Succeed

*"It is impossible to achieve success while your
mind is set on failure"* –Saleem Bidaoui

Is *Pleasure* a means to an end or an end by itself? I've read numerous books that dealt with the concept of pleasure as an end rather than a means. Some books have a valid argument but maybe a shortsighted one. Nearly all of these books deal with the subject as if it is all we need to achieve in life. They ask questions like, "Why do we want money?", for example. The answer is given that we do not need money for what it is but for what it can do for us and that is to make us happy. That's absolutely fine! However, when we ask questions like, "Is humanity only about becoming happy?" Is that it...and then we die?

The answer to this question is there must be a deeper meaning and purpose to life beyond just being happy. For an erudite to think that life is merely about pleasure would give it little value. As it will be explained in this chapter, pleasure and pain are built-in mechanisms to help us maintain our survival. That is to say, pleasure and pain are means to a noble end we call "Survival of the Human Race" and we ought to examine it from this perspective.

Here is a provocative question: "Are we bodies with brains or brains with bodies?" A weird question, isn't it? You might say, "What difference does it make?" Well, it does as you will find out soon! To properly and credibly answer this question, however, let me ask you another one. Genetically speaking, "What is our ultimate goal on earth as a species?" Have you ever thought of this question before? The answer to this question is "Survival". Think about it. Survival is the only 24 hour job we have, and the job of survival is all we do in life. We eat, drink, seek shelter, get married, work, buy, sell, and even kill just to survive. Don't we?

The key to understanding the roots of our behaviour and why we are deeply attracted to things such as money and sex is the following:

Whatever we do in life, we do it to survive. Survival is the main motivator behind all of our intentions, behaviour, and actions.

Hardware Vs. Software

Survival is our instinctual goal and only game in life. That is, all of our intentions, motivation, behaviour, and actions stem from our will to survive. We are hardwired that way and we do not even have to think about it.

Using computer jargon though, our instinct is part of our biological "Hardware" which is highly sophisticated and we have no control over it, whatsoever. Our hardware includes our body, brain, heart, soul, intuition, and instinct. Said differently, our hardware is anything that we do not have any control over and no choice but to accept it "As is". Trying to tamper with the instinctual part of our hardware, for instance, is as if we are trying to make a chick look for her mother's breast once it hatches from the egg. It is never going to happen, right? The same is true with our hardware.

12

Our "Software", on the other hand, is totally the opposite. It is under our control and we can program it and re-program it any way we want. Our biological software includes our thinking processes, perception, behaviour, mood, attitude, self-confidence, self-image, and so on. These are totally under our control and we do set them to achieve success...or failure. Yes, we do program them to fail on a regular basis if we want to and we do not have to look too far for the proof. We meet people who do this to themselves everyday.

But why am I telling you all of this? Simply because most people get mixed up between their *fixed* "Hardware" and their *programmable* "Software". Yes, we can program and reprogram our software, but not the hardware that's better known as our "human nature". Our hardware is survival-ready. Without it, you wouldn't have lived long enough to read this book. If so, then it is success-ready. Said differently, you cannot survive unless you succeed in doing so in every second of your life. Therefore, you are born to succeed and your initial failures are nothing but your training drills to teach you *how* to survive. This is extremely important for you to understand before you proceed and I urge you to go through it one more time if you're still not sure about what the difference between the two are.

Success or failure in life, however, is largely a matter of programming your *software*. The irony is, almost all of those who fail and call themselves "Total Failures" blame their *hardware* for their fiasco. Blaming the hardware for our debacles is just like cursing the driver for taking us to a destination of our own choosing. Ridiculous, yet absolutely true!

In this book I will strive to show you the real capacity of your own "hardware", the unlimited potential of your "software", and how to re-program yourself for *constant* success. It is never the "hardware" that holds you from reaching your "True Potential". It is entirely a matter of self-programming (*software*) that will either take you to Mars or will make sure you go nowhere in life.

Eternity Vs. Extinction

Now when it comes to survival, there is the highest point of survival and the lowest point. Obviously, the highest point of survival is to live forever, and the lowest point is to cease to exist at all.

On a spectrum, therefore, the highest form of survival is *"Eternity"*. Does it mean that we would love to be immortal? Well, look at all three heavenly books, the Torah, the Bible, and the Qur'an, and see what they are about. Eternity is our reward for being, and doing, good on earth, isn't it? Not to mention that many people think in those terms and work relentlessly to make it achievable in life. Billions of dollars exchange hands each year just from selling products and concepts that promise us younger looks, healthier bodies, more vitality, and a stretched lifespan. These products and concepts range from anti-wrinkle creams, to better sex, memory, and so on.

Can we achieve immortality? Some people are motivated to achieve eternity in life and this will lure many people to invest in anything that will promise them this dream! The point is, we are innately motivated to move towards this ultimate reward and we become excited about anything that will help us move in that direction.

Now if *eternity* is the highest form of survival, then obviously the lack of survival would be at the other end of the spectrum. That is to say, the less we succeed in life, the more we feel we are slipping toward uncertainty, the more prone to sickness we become, and the more we feel we are moving towards *"Extinction"*. Anytime we feel we are not winning the game of life, we automatically feel we are losing enthusiasm, sense of achievement, joy, and security. Consequently, we feel upset, miserable, and hopeless.

Now let me further clarify the concept of eternity and extinction before leaving it to mis-interpretation. Eternity and extinction are dealt with in here as a *direction* in life rather than a *destination*. What do I mean by that? As we all know, we live in a world of opposites. We have in and out, day and night, success and failure, happiness and misery, and so on. It is impossible for anyone to be in any two opposite directions at the same time. For example, it is impossible for you to be going North and South at the same moment in time. It's impossible for you to be happy and miserable at the same time. It is either/or. By the same token, we either move in the direction of eternity, or extinction. In Toronto, for example, we have the second busiest highway in the world known as the 401. The 401 starts in Windsor, Ontario, and stretches all the way to Cornwall, Ontario, which is approximately 1000 kilometres long. From Toronto, Windsor is "West" and Cornwall is "East". That is, every time I hop on that highway, either I travel "West", or I travel "East". Now does that mean that every time I use that highway I am going either to Windsor or to Cornwall? Of course not! It simply means that either I am going "West", or I am going "East", and for whatever distance I may choose. Well, the same is true with eternity and extinction. They are merely directions in our lives. When we move toward eternity, it means we are moving toward happiness, success, achievement, and fulfillment. When we move towards extinction, however, it means we are moving towards misery, helplessness, sickness, and ultimately death.

Therefore, the more we move towards eternity, the more successful and happy we are, the more control we have over our lives, and the more we can move toward a better life. Conversely, the more we feel we have no control over our lives, the more we feel that we are involuntarily moving in the direction of our extinction. That is to say, the healthier and more successful we are, the happier and wealthier we can be and the more we can move toward stretching our survival and lifespan. The less we can achieve this on the other hand, the more we feel we cannot achieve such a thrill, the more we feel hopeless, and the more we feel we are slipping towards uncertainty. This undesired feeling of helplessness will affect our health, mood, attitude, decisions, and eventually bring about chronic illnesses, sickness, misery, and pain into our lives.

Plain and simple, this is how every human being thinks, feels, and acts upon.

Anything we do is merely an attempt to move ourselves *toward* "Eternity" and/or *away from* "Extinction".

This innate desire to move ourselves in one direction or away from the other is the radar of our hardware and it applies to all aspects of our lives. Hence, our feelings of *pleasure* stem from anything that will move us towards securing basic necessities of life, and anything that can help us achieve this will bring us the feeling of pleasure.

In other words, we seek pleasure because it helps us survive, and to survive is pleasure by itself. The feeling of pain, on the other hand, comes from anything that could compel us to move toward extinction, such as, un-employment, poverty, uncertainty, lack of security, and sickness. Anything that can or even might move us in this direction will bring us anxiety, stress, the feeling of in-security, and pain.

Needless to say, the more we focus our attention toward eternity the more we feel hopeful and happy. The more we focus our attention towards extinction the more we feel hopeless, helpless, and miserable. Again, this feeling is built-in, genetic, and we can do nothing about it. As such, we spend our whole lives minute-by-minute and day-by-day running after two fundamental goals: We either try to move *toward* eternity, and/or try to move *away from* extinction. Said differently, we only try to move toward what brings us *Pleasure* and away from anything that could bring us *Pain,* and nothing else. Any decision we make, big or small, is just to move us in one of these two directions.

Here's human behaviour compressed into one sentence:

Whatever we do in life is either to gain *Pleasure* or to avoid *Pain.*

Just think of any decision you made in the last forty-eight hours and ask yourself, "Was this decision to make me move towards eternity, or just to avoid moving towards extinction?" That is, were you trying to gain the pleasure of moving toward eternity, or were you trying to avoid the pain of slipping toward extinction?

The answer will always be: either/or, regardless of what it is. Be it a visit to your doctor, buying a bike, lipstick, or a trip to the moon, and I'll prove it to you very soon. In a nutshell then, that is all we do in life and this is what "Human Behaviour" all about.

Reactive Vs. Proactive

Okay, so far we talked about some of our hardware's built-in mechanisms that were meant to help us survive. Now let's take it one-step further and briefly talk about the software, or the inception of our programming, if you will.

As humans, we've been given an apparatus like no other creature in this universe. Unlike any living thing, this apparatus gives us the ability to think and make choices. These choices take an active role in creating the software that includes our mood, character, conduct, and everything else that comes with it.

Indeed, our choices are the programmers of our minds and the architects of our destinies.

Anytime we *choose* to move toward eternity, however, we would be using a "*Pro-active Mode*" of thinking. And, anytime we choose to move away from extinction, we would be using a "*Reactive Mode*" of thinking. In other words, we normally act either by "*Choice*", or by "*Necessity*". What do I mean by that? Well, there is a huge difference between doing something to succeed and win, and doing something just not to fail or lose. There is a huge difference between, "I can and will achieve whatever I want in life" and, "Just let me have any job to get by and survive." Do you see the difference between these two statements? One depicts a "*Proactive*" mindset, and the other portrays a "*Reactive*" mindset. One is about focusing on moving toward eternity, and the other one is about moving away from extinction.

Needless to say, the difference between these two modes of thinking is one of the most crucial attributes of successful and unsuccessful people. Successful people focus entirely on moving toward eternity and obviously this is done by *"Choice"*, and unsuccessful people focus on how not to slide toward extinction thus do things by *"Necessity"*. As such, successful people will keep on moving upward, and unsuccessful people will stay occupied with how not to slide downward. One will continuously work on achieving their goals, and the other one will spend his/her life putting out fires.

Do you feel the difference between these two mind-sets? This is what might seem as a small difference, but definitely it makes a big difference in our lives. To give you an example, with all due respect to every human being though, take a "Doctor" and a "Dishwasher". Whom do you think acts by choice, and who acts by necessity? Obviously, the doctor acted by choice and that's why he or she is a doctor, and the dishwasher acted out of necessity and that is why he will not do any better.

Still not sure of what I am saying? Okay, being given a better alternative, would a dishwasher jump into this profession by choice? I doubt it! Did you ever hear some one saying, "When I grow-up, or when I graduate, I am going to be a dishwasher?" Being given the opportunity to choose, which one do you think people will pick as their first choice, and which one as a last resort? It's obvious, isn't it?

The point is, we all get caught in a reactive mode once in a while. Sometimes we have to do things out of necessity. To put food on the table and to keep a roof over our heads, that is. Stagnation and failure in life, however, come from being stuck in that mode. That is to say, maintaining a re-active stance simply means we are going nowhere in life. We are just *re-acting* to it, and reacting to it rather than being proactive also means we just gave-up or quit on our major goals and dreams in life.

The High-Standards Factor

Do you know that we are innately born with high-standards? High-standards are conducive to our survival, therefore, an integral part of our hardware and the root of our motivation. Without high-standards we would have still been living in caves and there would have been no need to advance in life! Just ask any child about what they want to be or do when they grow up and they will instantly demonstrate this fact. We're born with high standards, but unfortunately some of us voluntarily lower the bar of hope and success for ourselves one notch at a time until our self-esteem, confidence, and newly set standards are so low we are willing to accept whatever life has to offer, and which in most cases is not much. Have you ever been there? I've been there and I am sure you know someone who's been, or is still, there.

In summary then, success is about thinking entirely and moving adamantly in the direction of eternity and by doing so we naturally experience pleasure and sense of fulfillment. Moreover, failure is about getting caught-up in a reactive mode of thinking and by doing so we experience misery, discomfort, and sorrow simply because deep inside we know that we are not achieving anything significant in our lives. We are just reacting to it, and by incessantly doing so we would be acting in contrast to the high-standards we are born with.

The Three Necessities Of Life

Okay, we just talked about the mental, or the intangible, aspect of survival. Now let's touch upon the physical, or the tangible, aspect of it! Here is a question that is fundamental to our existence: What are some of the tools we *need* to be able to move toward eternity, and where the lack of these tools will force us to move toward extinction? To be able to move toward eternity we mainly need to achieve and secure three things that I call *"The Three Fundamental Necessities of Life"*:

1. **Money**
2. **Safety**
3. **Procreation**

Think about it. What is life all about? Money, safety, and sex, right? What is TV all about? Same thing! What is the News all about? Crime, wars, fires, jobs, the economy, and so on. What are the most successful programs on TV all about? Power, money, crime, wars, love, sex, etc. What is music all about? Money and love! Now, why do women buy lipstick for example? To look good, or better, and this has a lot to do with jobs and nesting, among other things. Why do people get married? Mainly to feel connected and to start a family. Where does the survival of mankind start? It starts and resumes with the process of procreation. Why do we buy a house, an alarm system, and insurance policies? To feel safe and secure.

I can go on and on and anyway you put it, it boils down to *"Money"*, *"Safety"*, and *"Procreation"*. We all feel compelled to move towards these and we will do anything to avoid losing them and for all of the reasons mentioned earlier. It is obvious that when we are deprived of these three things life becomes unbearable simply because we intuitively feel that we are moving towards extinction and this is the last thing we want to experience. All said and done, money, safety, and procreation, help pave the road to life's progression; nonetheless, they lubricate the process of moving smoothly toward eternity. Needless to say, lack of these paves the road to misery, anguish, and eventually to extinction.

Again, all we do in life is merely an attempt to secure these necessities, or try to avoid losing them. If you ask yourself, "Why am I reading this book?" it boils down to securing one or more of these necessities. It is either to gain the pleasure of achieving success, or more of it, and/or to avoid pain and whatever may come with it, and nothing else.

We all want:

a) A good job, or business, that will enable us to put food and other necessities of life on the table,
b) A safe environment to sustain life, and...
c) To establish a family that will carry our genes, and wealth if it exists, to the next generation. Keeping the family name alive, that is. And this is only one form of achieving eternity.

The Other Dimension

Does eternity have a different dimension other than pro-creation and keeping the family name alive? Think about it. Did the pharaohs, Sun Tzu, Confucius, Aristotle, Marcus Aurelius, Graham Bell, Marie Curie, Thomas Edison, Henry Ford, Margaret Thatcher, Bill Gates, Tiger Woods, and many, many other great men and women achieve some form of eternity? I think they did! All great people attain a form of eternity that I call: *"Eternity by Achievement"*. Thus, eternity is multi-dimensional. It can be achieved either by passing on our genes to the next generation, or by achievement, positive or negative.

We normally think of achievement as a positive outcome that benefits a person, a community, a nation, or mankind in general. However, when a thief commits a grand theft, what does he/she call their outcome, if succeeded? It is an achievement, but definitely a negative one. What do you think he/she calls it? They call it opportunity of a lifetime! History recent and ancient has documented the names of those whom achieved things we may call ruthless, or victorious. Whether we like it or not, dragging a nation to war remains an achievement registered by history, and history is the documented form of such an achievement, good or bad.

The Love Of Money

Is our love of money genetic? I strongly believe that money, just like mating, is engrained in our hardware as a means to survival. If so, then it becomes as an indispensable tool that we cannot survive without, especially during this time and age.

Money is not a choice. It is a must. But must be morally acquired, managed, saved, and spent.

It's an absolute necessity and must be morally pursued and acquired simply means we must not be too passive about generating it, or too possessive to the point where we hurt others in the process! It is unfortunate that some people out there pursue money cunningly, viciously, and aggressively to the point where they are willing to do whatever it takes to satiate their excessive greed of it. Well, that is not what I am talking about in here. There is always the right way to make and enjoy money, and there is the wrong way to have it. The right way is about enjoying the journey while you are on your way to success.

The wrong way is to focus on the destination and how to get there by any means. The wrong way is to think of money as a means to power rather than to enjoy life, do well, and help others in this world. The wrong way is to focus on how to make money and neglect everything else in your life just for the sake of having more of it.

There are people who put tremendous time and effort to succeed then get hung up on what I call the "Just One More Million Syndrome!" Do you know a successful person who does not spend quality time with his family just for the sake of making more money? That is not what money and life are all about! Life is about balance. It's about dealing with one aspect of your life without losing sight of the other. It's about the joy of making money and being there for your family at the same time, that is. It's about having leisure time in the process and giving some to those who need it most at the same time. Money is a means to a *better* quality of life, not an end by itself. That's what money is for and life is all about. This is real balance and success that lead to happiness.

> *"Money is a terrible master but an excellent servant."*
>
> – P. T. Barnum

Money Is Not Important!

Some people say that money is not too important. For those who believe in this please let's not fool ourselves by saying that money is not important. Money means survival.

It is as simple as that! T. Harv. Eker mentioned in his book, *"Secrets of the Millionaire Mind"*, that when someone says, "Money is not that important", all they are saying is, "I could not make it so far and this is just my excuse" which simply translates to "I am broke!"

The love of money is engrained in our genes and we all love it!

Whether we admit it or not, money is an indispensable tool that greatly influences the level of our welfare and survival. Unfortunately, some people cannot generate enough to become financially independent and as such put themselves in a state of denial just to alleviate their agony and then they go out and preach to the whole world that money is not that important. Yes, money is absolutely and undeniably very important to our survival and make no mistake about it! Just leave the notion of "It's not too important" to monks, if this is not your ultimate goal in life. Again, there is a huge difference between "It's not too important" and "How can I become financially self-sufficient", right?

The First Layer

Now here is a fundamental question that will lay-down the first layer in the foundation of your success. It's brief and simple, yet subtle and profound:

Are we well equipped, or ill equipped, for survival?

What do you think? If you said, "Yes, we are well-equipped", you are absolutely right. But be careful with what you just admitted to yourself! If you said, "Yes", then you just confessed to yourself that you have all the tools you need to succeed in life.

> *"Just like salmon, we are genetically programmed to swim upstream. The only difference is that we have the choice not to".* Unknown

Genetically, we are programmed to move upward in life, to survive, succeed, and towards eternity. If you are sceptical about your capacity to achieve success, this book will demonstrate to you time and again that you are capable, well equipped, and ready for success! As for those who think in terms of, "I don't have what it takes", I will show you that we all have much more than what it takes to be and have whatever we want in life and all we have to do is to claim it. Easier said than done? No, it is not, unless you are a C.M.I. (*Certified Mentally Ill*) person, of course. Here is a scientific fact that has been tested and proven hundreds of times:

If you are mentally normal, then you are utterly capable!

That is, whether you have an average IQ, or above average, there is absolutely nothing wrong with you and you can achieve anything you may desire simply because you already have all the tools you need to get you there.

Let me tell you a little secret:

There is a huge difference between "I *can*, but don't know how" and "I *can't*, thus why bother".

Do you see the difference between these two mindsets? This is another fundamental distinction between successful and unsuccessful people. Which one do you normally contemplate? It does make all the difference, dude! To think that *you can* will consciously and unconsciously put your brain in search for the "how". You will utilize all of your senses to act as a radar for opportunities that will help you achieve your goals. If you think you cannot, nothing else within you will, and as such you'll become oblivious to many good things happening around you.

As you read along, you'll discover that everything is interconnected either to help you succeed, fail, or something in between, depending on your belief system. You'll also learn that what you are today is not coincidental at all. When they say, "Life's what you make it", it is literally just that and there's nothing random about it.

Your Primary Tool

Now let's go back to the body/brain question. Do you still remember that question? Just in case you don't, let me ask it to you again: *"Are we brains with bodies or vice versa?"* So what do you think? Are you still not sure about the answer? To get you somewhere, let me ask you another question:

What are animals' primary tool for survival? Is it their body, or is it their brain? I am sure you'll agree with me that it is mainly their body that helps them to survive. "Survival of the Fittest" is the law of the land in their kingdom, isn't it? In their world, if you are not physically fit, you will be a good meal to those who are.

Now in our world, especially in this day and age, what is our primary tool for survival? Is it our body, or is it our brain? Obviously, it is mainly our brain that helps us survive, right? Even if you are a blue-collar-worker nowadays, you still have to rely on your mental faculty to cope with the technology and the sphere of change that is taking place around us every day. Therefore, it is our brain, and not our body, that distinguish us from animals and make us superior to everything in this universe. In general, our bodies are no longer our primary tool for survival. Plain and simple, we are living in an era of total mental dependence. Nowadays, the level of our success, or lack of it, is a matter of how we develop our brains, program them, and utilize them.

The body/brain question was not to provoke an argument as much as it was to emphasize the significance of our brains in our lives today. You might say, "What is so significant about this? We all know that!" Actually, what's significant about the whole thing has to do with the next two questions and how you handle them.

Here's the first one:

1.   *How much do you invest in your most important asset* (your brain) *in comparison to everything else in your life?*

Like, do you invest in your brains' well-being and growth as much as you do on clothes, vacation, or plasma TVs, for example? If you said "No", don't worry! You're not alone, and hopefully by the time you finish reading this book you'll change your mind about what your brain could do for you and how you can nurture it!

Let's see how you're going to handle the second question:

2.   *Do you know how your brain really works and how to get the best and the most out of it?*

Very few people can say "Yes" to this question. If you belong to the majority, however, then let's talk about your brain's *"Operations Manual"*, if you will. Let's see why some of us may, or may not, succeed and how you can achieve the success and happiness that you've always dreamt of having.

In the next chapter I will talk about a few physical features of the brain and then move on to discuss a few fundamental attributes that are relevant to your success. Carry on!

Chapter 2

Your Brain
Your Success

"Your reality is nothing but the lens that reflects back what you focus on. Change what you focus on, and you change your reality." –Saleem Bidaoui

Nothing is more fascinating than the brain. Look around you and you will instantly realize its power. From the pyramids of Egypt to the Space Station revolving around the earth, it never ceases to demonstrate its splendour. Now look internally and contemplate your own complexity. Think of how your brain handles and delegates every single cell and organ in your body, not to mention the sophisticated pharmacy at its disposal. Indeed, the brain is the most potent piece of blubber in the universe and it is located right in between your ears. It can take you to where no man has ever gone before, or it can orchestrate your failure and destruction with precision depending on whether you are riding it, or it is riding you.

Knowing more about your brain's functions and how it pursues something to make it real, or how it may deliberately neglect and overlook certain things that could be vital to your success, is what you are about to venture in. What you are about to read may not only change the way you look at yourself, but also at life itself.

In this chapter, I will briefly talk about the physical structure of the brain then explain the impact of these parts on our lives. You will soon discover that this structure is much more than just physical or random. Moreover, by knowing more about your brain will put you in charge of many aspects of your life that you may have thought were beyond your control. So let us start with a few facts.

Brain Structure

Although the brain has many inter-dependent parts and these parts create a synergy within our body, in this book I will only mention the ones that directly influence our behaviour and are relevant to our success.

- **It's About 3 lbs. (1.4 kgs)**

  The brain is approximately 2% of our total body weight. This 2%, however, consumes about 20% of our total energy and 40% of the nutrients we take into our body. The brain is a guzzler! It needs a continuous supply of fuel to keep it running well. What does this mean? Carry on to find out.

- **The Brain Has Four Major Parts**

  a. *The Top Part*

  The top part is that convoluted or wrinkled portion of the brain known as the cortex. This is your "Thinking Brain". This part is further divided into the left & right hemispheres, and it includes the conscious mind and the sub/un-conscious mind.

  b. *The Middle Part*

  This part is known as the mid-brain, or the limbic system. The two parts that are relevant to us within the limbic system are the hippocampus, which is the distribution center of our memories, and the amygdala, which is among other things the distribution center of our emotions.

  c. *The Bottom Part*

  The bottom part is better known as the brain-stem, or the reptilian brain. This is the instinctual part of us and this is where our "fight, flight, or freeze" mechanism is located. It is also called the reptilian brain because that is the only part that reptiles have in their skull. As such, if you have a reptile as a pet, please do not bother trying to teach them their name or a few tricks. They will never get it! They have no thinking brain, no emotions, and no memory, thus cannot learn. In humans though, there is something unique in this part of the brain. It is the size of your little finger and it is called the R.A.S. (*Reticular Activating System*).

d. The Bottom Rear Part

Right behind the brain-stem there is the cerebellum. Does this part have anything to do with your success or failure? This part is your autopilot or the automatic trigger of your success, or failure, depending on how you train it. You train it to fail, and it will automatically trigger behaviours that will ensure just that. It's automatic and you don't even have to think about it.

Brain Power

How powerful is your brain, do you think? Before I explain that, let me first tell you how your brain cells interact with each other. As you know, brain cells constantly communicate with each other and that's what keeps you thinking and alive. However, when they do communicate, brain cells don't physically touch one another to perform this task. There is a very tiny gap between brain cells called the synapse. This gap is filled with CSF (*Cerebral Spinal Fluid*) which is mainly made out of water. The cells communicate with each other by firing minute electrical charges and chemicals across the synapse, or from the *sending* part of one cell to the *receiving* end of another. This process of firing electrical and chemicals charges from one cell to another is known as the "*Electro-Chemical Process*" and that is how we think!

Taste Buds Power

On our tongues, however, there are approximately 10,000 taste buds. Within each taste bud there are about 50 receptor-cells similar to our brain cells. When these cells fire similar electro-chemical messages between them, they provide us with the ability to recognize the tastes that we experience every time we put something in our mouths. Having said that, then how many receptor cells do we have on our tongues? We have around 500,000 receptor cells (10,000 taste buds x 50 receptor cells). These 500,000 receptor cells however are divided into four categories only:

1. *Sweet* receptor cells located at the front,
2. *Salty* receptor cells on both sides,
3. *Sour* tasting receptor cells in the middle, and
4. *Bitter* tasting receptor cells at the back.

We experience a specific taste depending on the frequency of firing and the specific chemical reaction of each type. Thus, the process of tasting is also an electro-chemical reaction that takes place in our mouth every time we put something in it.

Hypothetically speaking though, let's say you put something in your mouth and the bitter tasting receptor cells start firing at 1 cycle per second, the salty receptor cells at 3 cycles per second, the sweet receptor cells at 7 cycles per second, and the sour tasting receptor cells fire at 17 cycles per second. That specific combination is interpreted to you by your brain as the taste of a lemon. With minor variation in this blend and it becomes the taste of an orange, tangerine, and so on.

As you can imagine, there are literally millions of different tastes that we can experience just from four types of cells. Only four types of taste buds, a handful of chemical exchanges, a specific firing sequences, and we get millions and millions of different tastes. Amazing isn't it?

Are you following me so far? If not, please go back and read this paragraph again. This is extremely important for you to grasp before you proceed.

Neuro-Success

Now listen carefully to what I am going to say because what you are about to read will change your life. Our brains have four firing cycles:

Alpha, Beta, Delta, and Theta. These are known as our brain waves and we experience all of these waves during a 24-hour period.

Our brains, however, don't just have 500,000 cells with merely 4 functions like the tongue, but more than a 100,000,000,000 brain-cells, or neurons, with hundreds of trillions of connections to other brain cells that relatively work and communicate on the same principle as our tongues. So can you imagine the magnitude of what your brain can do? That's how powerful your brain is…if you want to use it. I say that because what you do with your billions of brain-cells and trillions of connections is an absolute *choice*.

What your billions of neurons "chemically" exchange, or deliberately refrain from exchanging, intentionally hold back that is, and the frequency of their firing is what literally makes you.

Everything about you, whether you like it or not, lies in *how* this electro-chemical process is working. This process totally controls your intelligence, decisions, motivation, enthusiasm, behaviour, mood, health, appetite, sleeping patterns, and energy, to name a few. Unless you take active measures to control it, you're not going to be happy with how it runs things because as powerful as it is the brain is lazy and loves to take shortcuts. In many cases it normally takes the wrong shortcuts when left on its own.

From now on always keep in mind that your whole life and everything about you is the by-product of *how* your electro-chemical process is functioning. When you feel depressed, for example, you feel this way because your brain cells are exchanging chemicals that are making you feel depressed, such as cortisol, and it is holding back the release of hormones that could make you feel happy, calm, or at least normal, such as serotonin.

Anti-depressant drugs, for example, all they do is alter this electro-chemical process by fooling the brain to release pleasure hormones into your blood stream and hold back depressing hormones. Does it mean that I am promoting these drugs? In fact it is totally the opposite and, in this case, I am talking about normal people with no medical or mental history. When normal people start using those drugs, they become addicted to those drugs, and for life. The problem is that many people think they are not normal anymore and life is overwhelming and as such they must have those drugs to make them feel normal again. They resort to such drugs as an easy way out despite the fact they have natural cures within their skull. I am neither a doctor, nor a psychiatrist, to comment on this issue. No doubt about it, there are cases where those drugs are needed and I am not arguing with that.

My point is, when we insist on taking the wrong highway everyday and consequently don't get where we want to go, it is not surprising that we need such drugs to calm us down. Some of us create our own stress and like everything else in our lives, we seek the solution outside of our body. To many people things must always come from external sources. Not knowing that success and happiness, for example, must be nurtured and come from within first, and unless they do so, they are not going to experience it. Further, not knowing that this kind of thinking will eventually create a stress that may need medical attention. Think about it. Happiness only exists in your mind and all else is merely an accessory to it. The paradox is, many people say they'll be happy when they succeed. Well, here's another reality check:

Unless you are happy first, you're not going to succeed.

Having said all of that, is it possible to control our own electro-chemical process and drastically change our lives without using drugs? Yes, it is very possible to do so. This whole book is nothing but an attempt to help you streamline this process and put you in control of your life. You won't believe how easy it is to do so. Just hang on and I'll get you there!

Elements Of Manifestation

Some people literally stifle their brain cells then go out and claim to the whole world that they are incompetent. Those are the ones that tell themselves and everyone around them in one way or the other that "They don't have what it takes to succeed". Neuro-science has proven beyond a shadow of a doubt that you can be whomever you choose to be. How can you achieve that? Just look around you. What do you see? Buildings, highways, cars, airplanes, computers, and an enormous number of other inventions!

How did these come to reality? Everything that has been achieved, or will be achieved, come to be reality by investing in what? Think about it. Anything we want to manifest into our lives must involve three fundamental elements:

1. **Thought**
2. **Time**
3. **Energy**

For example, when you invest ten years of your life in studying medicine, what will you manifest into your life? Becoming a doctor, right? Now, when you spend ten years of your life watching TV, what will you manifest into your life? Ten years of useless entertainment that no one really needs. Said differently, when you spend ten years of your life on nothing, you'll manifest nothing!

The bittersweet fact is, how you used your thoughts, time, and energy in the past brought you to where you are today. How you use your thoughts, time, and energy *today* will be manifested into your life tomorrow. It's a matter of Cause & Effect. Doesn't take too much to figure that out, does it? The irony is, most people want to become financially independent while watching TV in their spare time. Accordingly, they don't make progress to achieve the success they always dreamt of and then they come to you and talk about the stress that is haunting them day and night. No wonder!

Here are three crucial questions I want you to ask yourself and then ponder before you move on:

- *What kind of tomorrow do I want?*
- *Where do I want to see myself in ten years from now?*
- *What shall I do today to have a better tomorrow?*

If you want your life to stay the same, just do nothing and you'll sustain the status quo, guaranteed. Conversely, if you wish to have a different lifestyle and be something and somewhere else in the future, you must invest in the "Elements of Manifestation", *today*.

Always remember this:

Your today is whatever you invested in yesterday and your tomorrow will be whatever you invest in it today.

Again, just look around you and you'll notice that everything you see involved an investment of thought, time, and energy before and during it's transformation into reality. Anything you see or can think of involved these three elements in a focused form, however. That is to say, the more you focus these three elements on some-thing specific such as success per se, the more you'll get what you focused on. The more you focus these three elements on nothing, the more you'll get nothing too.

<u>One caveat:</u> The more you focus your thoughts, time, and energy on *what's NOT working in your life*, the more you'll get what you focus on. The more you focus on what you do not want in your life, the more you will get that as well. The more you focus on your problems rather than solutions, the more you are stuck with those problems. This is just the way your brain works.

Bottom line: Whatever you invest in today will show up in your life tomorrow, be it positive or negative. Life is not capricious. There are "Laws of Success", and "Laws of Failure" as well. When you stick to the rules of one, you'll seldom get the other. Thought, time, energy, and the intensity of your focus is one aspect of either playing it by the laws of success, or the laws of failure!

"Success has a price, you pay it and it's all yours!"
– Unknown

These three elements are the price! Are you willing to pay it? If you automatically said "Yes", then you are on your way to a better life. If you said, "Well, I love to… but", then you are not ready to change and nothing will happen in your life until you do. Plain and simple!

Anatomy of Thought

So far we talked about the three elements of manifestation and their influence on what we get in life. Now let's talk about the most fundamental element of these three and that is "Thought".

As you know, thought is generated by the brain. What you may not know, however, is that your brain cells are extroverts. Say that again! Literally, our brain cells can only survive and flourish when they reach out and socialize with other brain cells in the neighbourhood of our skull. What do I mean by that? Earlier, I said that some people stifle their brain cells then go out and claim to the whole world that they are incompetent. Conversely, our brain cells can regenerate and survive for a long time when they branch out and socialize with other cells. If they don't due to lack of engagement, they may atrophy as a result. Hence, *mental activity* revives brain cells and lack of it kills them.

Having said that, then what stimulates our brain cells to go out and socialize and what prevents them from dying? Here's another little secret that's vital to your success:

Among other things, the process of "Learning" keeps our brains happy, healthy, vibrant, and alive!

That is to say, any time you attempt to learn some-thing new your brain cells get excited and jump to your aid by forming a network of dedicated brain cells to help you succeed in that specific process.

Unfortunately, some people think that the process of learning ends the day they graduate. Formal education is essential but to think that you need no more of it after you finish school is a one-way ticket to mediocrity, stagnation, and maybe failure. The world we live in is changing faster than ever before and unless you keep abreast of the things that are relevant to you, at least, your chances of a decent living will get slimmer by the hour even if it may not be apparent to you at the time. Just don't wait until you find yourself obsolete and then try to jump on the last cabin of the train of life. It is very crowded in there.

The Four Attributes

Okay, so far we discussed a few physical features of the brain starting from its weight and all the way down to the function of one neuron. Now let's talk about four fundamental attributes that are crucial to your success:

1. The Brain Stores No Energy

Unlike the body, the brain stores no energy. Okay, what is significant about this? Earlier I mentioned that our brain consumes 20% of our energy and 40% of the nutrients you take into your body. Now I am saying that the brain stores no energy. Obviously, unless there is a continuous supply of energy, the brain's performance will suffer. Therefore, if you skip breakfast or lunch, for example, will your brain function at its peak performance during that time? No, it will not simply because your brain, as well as your body, will be starving for energy and it is not there. What will happen as a result? Your aptitude will drop in relative amount to the level of energy you need.

So what's the trick here? In order for you to maintain a superior brain performance, you need to keep yourself *properly fed* and *hydrated* all day long. By properly fed I mean a candy bar or a donut will not do the job and we'll talk about nutrition in more detail in Part Two.

2. Has a Natural Negative Tendency

The brain has a negative tendency and that is mainly to protect you from danger. Without this tendency you'll cross the street with no regard for cars or trucks driving by and you wouldn't even question anything that is going on around you. In other words, without this tendency you'll become passive to your environment. Thus, this tendency is to help you anticipate danger and to prep you to take necessary precaution to protect yourself from danger.

This tendency though is the positive side of the story. The negative side of this story is when you are on autopilot, not consciously thinking, that is. Your brain's negative tendency will take over and you'll behave accordingly. This will not only affect your thinking process negatively, but also your decisions and actions. Meaning, when this happens, you'll un-consciously behave in agreement with your own programming almost all day long. Unless this programming is positive, your brain's negative tendency will not make your life any easier. So what is the remedy if you need different results in your life? The remedy is to develop *positive thinking habits* to balance this tendency. You don't want to eliminate this tendency because, as I said earlier, it is there to protect you from danger. You just need to balance it in order to bring about a healthy way of thinking into your daily routine.

3. **Equipped With a "Failure Mechanism"**

Just hold your horses! This doesn't mean that you are equipped to "fail". Rather, this mechanism is to help you learn, cope with, and adapt to your environment so you can easily succeed and survive. Any time you undertake a task and screw-up, so to speak, this mechanism kicks-in and gives feedback to specific portions of your brain that are associated with this specific task. As such, the brain will take corrective action and do a better job the next time you repeat the same action again. This is how you learn to ride a bicycle, ski, drive a car, write well, move the cup in precise motion to your lips, and everything else you do on a regular basis.

Now listen to this: When someone deliberately de-activates this mechanism, they'll deprive themselves from the opportunity to learn from that experience and the opportunity to correct their mistakes. What will happen when we don't learn from our mistakes?

We'll have the propensity to do the same mistake again, and again, and again, right?

Now I am sure you are wondering: if that's the case, how could anyone in his/her right mind de-activate this invaluable mechanism? That's simple and easy! Listen carefully to what I am going to say next because it's imperative to streamlining and controlling your electro-chemical process:

Any time you dodge responsibility, you de-activate your failure mechanism!

Any time you say, "It is he or she and not me", your failure mechanism goes to sleep because if it's not you, then your brain doesn't have to work on it and fix it at all. Subsequently, you don't learn from such an experience and you'll have the susceptibility to repeat the same mistake again. In the larger scheme of things, this will drastically minimize your chances of success because instead of automatically repeating a successful act, you'll spend more and more of your time putting out fires due to repetitive mistakes. Conversely, when you take responsibility for your actions no matter what the consequences may be, either your brain will save that experience as a "successful encounter" and make ready to use the next time you need it, or it will take corrective action to do a better job when it considers that experience as less than successful or perfect.

Hence, it's of supreme benefit for us to take responsibility for our actions simply because it's the only way we can improve and grow. Mind you, this mechanism is one of the most important keys to your success as you'll find out later.

4. Thinks In Pictures

If I say, "Think of a red apple", what will you see in your mind's eye? A red apple, right? You don't see the words "red apple". Even if you try to recall these words, you'll recall an image of these words. Again, it's just the way the brain works.

We communicate with *words*, but think in *pictures*.

If I say, "Tie your shoe lace", you'll recall the concept of "tying your shoe lace". You don't see the words. Moreover, we normally look up and to the left to *recall* an image and to right to *construct* an image. Having said that, can you find out if someone is lying just by watching their eye movement? Yes you can! All you have to do is figure out which side is for recall and which one is for constructing images and then notice their eye movement when they answer your questions.

Now does this concept of thinking in pictures have anything to do with your success? You bet it does! Just hang on and you'll find how powerful this concept is.

Chapter 3

Conscious Vs. Unconscious Mind

*"Thoughts shape character. Character dictates behaviour.
Behaviour creates destiny."* –Saleem Bidaoui

Many people get mixed-up between the functions of the conscious and unconscious mind. For example, which one do you think is more powerful, the conscious mind, or the unconscious mind? I am sure you have an opinion on that and I suggest you suspend your bias for now.

Let's go back to the brain structure and briefly talk about the top part or the thinking part of the brain. Earlier, I mentioned that this part is divided into two hemispheres, the *"Right Hemisphere"* and the *"Left Hemisphere"*. The left hemisphere of the brain deals with language, speech, mathematics, analysis, rational thinking, and so on.

The right hemisphere, on the other hand, deals with concepts, the big picture, daydreaming, imagination, creativity, music, and so on. When you listen to a song, for example, the lyrics will be processed on the left side of the brain, and the music itself will be processed on the right side of the brain. The right side of the brain handles the left side of the body, and the left side handles the right side of the body.

The Six Regions

In 1997 scientists at the University of Florida wanted to verify the functions of each hemisphere in action. They wanted to see with their own eyes that when we calculate, for example, the left side of the brain becomes active and not the right side of the brain. So they brought in about a hundred volunteers and, one by one, gave them an intravenous with a reduced radioactive material (*isotope*) that would act as tracer in the blood so the scientists could vividly see the activity of the brain on their monitors. Right after, they took each volunteer and put him/her into a PET-Scan (*Positron Emission Tomography Scanner*).

Since they were after the *thinking* processes of the brain and not the *automatic* functions of the brain and since most functions of the brain are always active, they filtered out all automatic functions of the brain from the scanner.

While each volunteer was in the scanner, they asked him or her to repeat to themselves, not out loud that is, the multiplication tables for number seven, for example. Just sit there and quietly calculate seven times one is seven, seven times two is fourteen, seven times three is twenty-one, and so on. Now if scientific theories were correct, which side of the brain would show activity and lit up on the monitor? The left side, right? Well, that's exactly what the monitor showed. Every volunteer was performing the mathematical problems on the left front side of their brain. However, something else that was totally unexpected also showed up on the screen at the same time. The scans also showed an activity in five other regions of the brain. Okay, what does this mean and what did the researchers discover for the first time in 1997? Scientists learned, and for the first time, that thinking takes place in six different areas of the brain and all at once. What are these six areas? To find out, scientists decided to take this experiment one-step further and they added a sedative into each volunteer's intravenous to put them to sleep while they were still performing their calculations. After the volunteer went to sleep, the only area that went off the monitor was the left front area of the brain while the other five areas remained lit. So what area do you think went off and what areas stayed on? The only area that went off after the volunteers went to sleep was the area of the conscious mind. Obviously, we can't go to sleep and remain conscious at the same time, can we? So what are the other five areas that remained active? The other five regions make the unconscious, or subconscious mind, and which never sleeps. If it sleeps, you're dead. Okay, what else did the scientists discover? Actually a lot! For all intents and purposes, let me lay-down only seven attributes of the conscious mind and seven attributes of the un-conscious mind that have great influence over your success, or failure.

When it comes to conscious verses unconscious mind I am not going to suggest to you which one is more powerful and fascinating. I'll leave that to your judgment. I do want you, however, to pay close attention to the solid contrast between the two because being able to identify these differences will put you in the driver's seat of your life. So let's briefly touch upon some attributes of the conscious mind first.

The Conscious Mind

As much as the conscious mind has power and advantages, it has many limitations as well. Let's find out about its superiority and some of its shortcomings.

1. **Analyzes, Plans, Judges, Accepts & Rejects**

   This part, which is located at the front part of the brain, controls and utilizes the "Awareness" part of us. Anytime we are aware of something, be it thinking, an action, or the surrounding, it is due to our conscious mind. Any time we can pay attention to, or focus on something, it is entirely due to that part of the brain.

2. Functions At 210 km/sec.

Is the conscious mind fast or slow? By scientists' standards, the conscious mind is very slow, especially in comparison to the unconscious mind which is eight hundred times faster. Now that's fast!

3. Can Hold 7 - 9 Bits Of Information

What is 7 bits of information? Your telephone number, for example. Phone numbers have been deliberately set to seven digits after phone companies consulted with psychologists in that regard. What is 9 bits of data? Your SIN (*Social Insurance Number*), if you are Canadian. More or less, that's how much information our conscious mind can hold at one time and which is not much at all. Okay, having said that, what does this tell us about the conscious mind so far?

The conscious mind has "No Memory"!

This is an extremely important piece of information. Just keep this in mind for now.

4. Can Only Entertain "One Thought"

Consciously, we can only focus on one thing at a time. Yes, we can think of five, ten, or as many issues as we want but we still have to stop thinking about one to start thinking about the other. We simply cannot think of two things at the same moment in time. If your mind is with what you are reading right now, and I hope it is, then it's impossible for you to be occupied with something else at this same moment. Mentally, you have to stop paying attention to what you are reading, even for a split second, to be able to think of something else. Thus,

We can only focus on one thing at a time!

5. Interacts With The Unconscious Mind

Because the conscious mind doesn't have memory, it always refers back to the unconscious mind to get the information it needs.

Let me give you an example of how this works. Let's say you went to the mall to buy a dress or a suit. You go into a store and the salesperson greets you then asks you for what you want. You tell him/her about what you're looking for and they bring a couple of dresses/suits for you to see and try on. Now, for simplification purposes, let's say that you have only two choices: Black or Blue. Your conscious mind cannot decide which one to choose simply because it has no memory thus has no reference to anything. As such, it will request input from the unconscious mind about the black...and the blue dress/suit. The unconscious mind will search its database, look for relevant information, and then tells the conscious mind that you already have a blue dress/suit. Mind you all of this searching happens in a fraction of a second and you look at the salesperson and say, "I prefer the black one. Let me try it on".

Okay, what does all of this mean? To begin with, it means that your conscious mind is like a very good CPU (*Central Processing Unit*) that is made for calculations and analysis, but not for storage or memory. Thus, without a hard-drive that can store all of your experiences this potent CPU can do nothing at all. What is your bio-hard-drive, or the seat of your memory, if you will? You got it! It's your unconscious mind. That's where everything about you is stored.

Okay, what's so crucial about this? Believe it or not, this is also of utmost significance to your success. When you understand how this works your life will not be the same anymore. This is one of the scientific secrets to happiness, motivation, and permanent success. How is that? Let me give you a quick example for now. When you need to get rid of a bad habit, can your conscious mind alone help you achieve that? You know the answer by now, don't you? That is, "No" it cannot be done by the conscious mind alone!

The irony is that most people depend entirely on their conscious mind to do this for them and that's exactly why they fail to achieve favourable and permanent results in their lives.

In summary, the conscious mind alone cannot bring about any changes in your life. It is where things start but without the unconscious mind it cannot be maintained and recalled because it has no memory. As such, it always refers back to the un-conscious mind for input before it can reach a conclusion. Just keep this in mind for now and I'll explain this success prerequisite in further details later on. The next attribute, however, may reveal it all.

6. **Holds The Key To Your "Willpower"**
Did you ever hear someone's saying, "I am going to quit smoking no matter what"? Every time someone says something like this they would be relying on their willpower. Willpower, however, is the *"Aggressive"* portion of your conscious mind. Now, is this good or bad? Actually, it's good because it initiates your desire to achieve things in your life.

Let me put it this way:

Your willpower is the ignition switch of your motivation.

As discussed earlier, willpower is part of the conscious mind that has no memory. Therefore, willpower alone cannot bring about long-term results due to that fact, especially if it's in conflict with the unconscious mind. Did I confuse you? Then let me give you another example. If you say, "I am going to quit smoking NOW!" or, "I'll become a non-smoker starting today", for example, and your subconscious mind is saying, "No, No, No, dear. In here — in the memory part that is — it says that you are a smoker". Guess who will win the day? Is it your conscious, or unconscious mind, do you think?

Here's the undisputed rule about this:

When the conscious mind and the un-conscious mind are in conflict, the un-conscious mind holds the key to long-term results.

If you're consciously saying, "I am going to quit smoking" and your subconscious mind, or bio-hard-drive is saying, "you are a smoker", you may succeed in doing it for a while in the short-run, that is. In the long run, however, you are still a "smoker" and your unconscious mind will do whatever it takes to enforce that *image*. It will keep on reminding you about it in many uncomfortable ways until you go back to your comfort-zone with regard to smoking and thus smoke again. That's why New Year's resolutions don't work, by the way. That's why some people cannot quit smoking, or lose weight. That's why fitness clubs are packed in January and near empty a couple of months later. People strictly use their willpower to get results. Willpower alone will not bring about long-term results and for all of the obvious reasons you know by now. That's why some may succeed for a while but eventually succumb to their old habits and there's a good reason for this. Having said that, can we achieve different results, permanently? Let's go to attribute # 7 to unveil another clue.

7. Programs The Unconscious Mind

Paradoxical as it may seem, the conscious mind will always be the programmer of your unconscious mind and this is the *"Smooth Talker's"* portion of the conscious mind in contrast to the *"Aggressive"* portion, or the opposite side of your willpower, if you will. It is as if the conscious mind has two strategies: a *"Push-Strategy"* and *"Pull-Strategy"*. Push-strategy is applied through willpower, and pull-strategy through the programmer/smooth talker.

As emphasized by Dr. Tom Miller, if you can think of your unconscious mind as a "horse", then this portion is the "rider". It trains the unconscious mind where to go on a regular basis, and with no further instructions or interference from the conscious mind. This portion trains the unconscious mind to do things on its own, that is. Why does it do so? To free up the conscious mind so it can handle other things.

Now, let's find out what the unconscious mind is all about.

The Sub/Un-Conscious Mind

The most important thing to remember about the un-conscious mind is that it's *"Error Free"*. Said differently, your unconscious mind will store and distribute data precisely as received. It does not forget or tamper with the information stored in its database and this has many implications. Let's find out what they are.

1. **Has An Unlimited Storage Capacity**

   Do you still remember what I said about the conscious mind, to that regard? The conscious mind has no memory, right? That's the kind of contrast I would like you to pay attention to. Now have you ever heard the notion that we only use about 10% of our brains? Well, there are two sides to this story. First, if we're talking about *"Storage Capacity"*, then this is untrue because we cannot even use 1% of our brain's capacity, even if we live to be 1000 years old and read every single book on earth during that time. So, in that sense don't worry, you'll never run out of memory. Secondly, if we're talking about *"Working Capacity"*, then this is also not true because we use most of our brain, non-stop. As I mentioned earlier, there are those who reduce this capacity by keeping their brains less engaged. A good example are those who watch TV for a long time everyday because during that time the brain is only at the receptive end and not too much thinking is involved in this process. In other words, unless TV is used for educational purposes, it is counter productive to your brain's growth and ought to be kept at minimum.

2. **Learns, Stores, Then Responds**

   What does it learn? The unconscious mind learns about every single bit of experience we go through in every waking moment of our lives and it's learning as you read these lines right now.

   What we have in memory is simply an accrual of that *learned* experience. We come to this world with zero memory. That's why babies can't see for a few days after birth, by the way. Right after a few days, however, they start gathering one experience after the other. This is mom, dad, bed, toy, room, and so on. Then as they grow older they learn this is good, bad, hot, cold, safe, unsafe, true, false, etc. That is to say, other than our survival built-in tools we did not come to this world equipped with any kind of knowledge or experience, did we?

Now I have a question for you: Can we accumulate any kind of experience without the assistance of our five senses? What do you think? Actually whether you said 'Yes' or 'No' you are right because there are two routes to gathering experience and both are essential to our personal programming, character, and success.

Let's examine these two:

a) **Actual Experience**

The first route is through *"Actual Experience"*, which is anything and everything that happens to us and around us on a daily basis. This task is solely franchised by our "Five Senses". Strictly handled by our senses, that is. It's what we see, hear, smell, touch (feel), and taste.

Now listen to this: although we build up our experience and references through our five senses, we don't have a direct encounter with what we call *reality*. What we experience at any moment in time is only a *presentation* by our senses to our brain and then our brain *re-presents* this information to us as it sees fit. Our senses only transfer scrambled raw-data to the brain and then the brain *re-assembles* this data and gives it a *meaning* based on previous experience, values, beliefs, and perception.

Therefore, we see what we see strictly because of our brain, and not because of what our eyes are seeing. Weird, isn't it? This is very important to keep in mind though!

Let me give you an example that we'll use later on: Did it ever happen to you that you're looking for something and it's right there in front of your eyes but you did not see it, at least for a moment?

This happens to all of us, doesn't it? Now let me ask you

this: Did your eyes see it? Of course it did! It's just for some reason your brain didn't want you to see it, and as such, you did not see it for a while.

Bottom line: Our *reality* at any moment in time is strictly based on what our brain is telling us, and not because of what our senses bring in to us. Our senses only present raw-data to our brain and then our brain *re*-presents to us as it finds appropriate. Well, **"Welcome to Reality!"**

Okay, what does this have to do with your success, you may ask? Wait until I show you how opportunities stand in front of your nose every single day and you wouldn't see them at all merely because of this factor. Is it starting to click? Great! If not, don't worry. I'll explain it in further detail later on. Now let's talk about the second and different kind of experience and that is:

b) **Synthetic Experience**

Paradoxically, the other experience that also shapes our reality is our *"Synthetic Experience"*. It is the experience we internally generate without any direct interference from our senses. Synthetic experience includes imagination, daydreaming, fantasizing, visualizing, and so on. It is a paradox because of how an *imagined* experience shapes our *reality*. Well, I believe that this experience is much more powerful than the actual one and I'll try to demonstrate that as we move along. Yes of course, *"Actual Experience"* is the root of our memory, but not necessarily the real driving force behind our lives. You might be surprised to know that our synthetic experience exerts more influence over our lives than the real one. The plain truth is the following:

> **You are who you are today mainly because of your synthetic experience.**

Now listen carefully to what I am going to say next about your synthetic experience in general, and your imagination in specific, because what you are about to read will change your life and here it is:

> Change the direction of your *imagination,* and you change your life.

You are who you are right now because of your imagination and the way you see yourself in your mind's eye on a regular basis and unless you alter your current vision of yourself to whatever you *wish to be* in life, scientifically speaking, it will be impossible for you to achieve a different out-come. That is to say:

> The more you see yourself the way you are right now, the more you are *stuck* with the way you are right now!

Your *imagination* creates your *reality* and I am going to prove it and then help you improve it. How's that? For now, however, let's go back and explain how the unconscious mind stores these experiences and then responds accordingly.

The unconscious mind learns by initially placing our current experience in short-term memory and then will decide whether to store this experience in long-term memory or delete it all together. A good example is when you drive on a two way street. In most circumstances, the second a car passes by you on the other side of the street your brain automatically deletes it from your memory. Why? The brain does this so you won't be overwhelmed by the magnitude of information that you are bombarded with every second. Unless this information is swiftly deleted, you would go insane in a matter of minutes, literally!

But how does the unconscious mind decide on what to keep and what to get rid of at any moment in time? Two important variables will determine all of that! Of course, there are many other variables involved such as *emotions* and *associations* but let's keep it simple for now and exclude those.

I. Spaced Repetition

The first variable is called "Spaced Repetition" and it takes place when something has been repeated many times at different occasions such as once in the morning, maybe again tomorrow, next week, and so on. That is, there is a time gap between one cycle of that action and another. Saying or doing something one hundred times in a row is not considered spaced repetition until it has been done more than once and at different time intervals. When this happens though, the brain considers the experience as a worthy piece of information and, as such, will save it in long-term memory. Advertisers are fully aware of this fact and they utilize this concept very well, by the way. Playing an ad over and over again is not a coincidence. They keep on spoon-feeding your unconscious mind with their product until it sinks in. Guess what you'll recall when you need something relevant? That product that you saw hundreds of times!

Is spaced repetition important to know about? Well, if someone keeps on repeating to themselves, now and, then something like *"I am not worthy"*, or *"I can never succeed"*, for example, will it be stored in their long-term memory? Yes it will.

II. Importance

The second variable that induces the unconscious mind to store a certain experience or a piece of information in long-term memory is its perceived importance. Anything that our unconscious mind marks as significant to us it will store it in long-term memory and if it's highly important it will place it in *"Rapid Recall Memory"* as well. If I ask you about your spouse, kids, or your parents' names, it's there. It is an *"Instant Recall"*! Why? Because these names are significant and mean something to you.

Now, if I ask you what did you have for dinner last October 16th, do you still remember what you had for dinner on that day? Highly unlikely! Why? Because for most of us that date is insignificant. As such, our brain will delete it in no time. However, if your anniversary or birthday is on that day and you celebrated it with your spouse somewhere special, most likely you will remember what you had for dinner that day, right? So can you see how the brain stores and/or deletes certain information? The brain by the way deletes much, much, more than it keeps and for all of the reasons mentioned earlier.

Now let's see what happens to the information we saved in memory. Again, the unconscious mind *learns, stores,* and then it *responds.* What does it respond with? It strictly responds with what has been stored in memory, and nothing else. The un-conscious mind is error-free and acts just like a robot or recorder. It does not judge what's in memory or tries to change it in any way. It simply follows orders to execute what has been instilled in there and no more or less.

Using computer analogy, the file you saved on your bio-hard-drive will be the only file your un-conscious mind can play back and work with. Are you starting to link things together now? Great! Now you know why you are what you are and why your life is the way it is. The plain truth is *we* create the status quo by what we plant in our un-conscious mind and if we don't like what we are seeing so far, we do have the control and power to change it.

3. **Always Says, "Yes 'Master' and Let Me Help You Live it!"**
   To whom does it say that? The unconscious mind is a very loyal servant to the conscious mind. As such, it will blindly obey its master and pass the instructions to your nervous system to act accordingly.

   Said differently, whatever your conscious mind embeds in the unconscious mind, positive or negative, good or bad, true or false, the unconscious mind will automatically attempt to bring it to life.

   A fundamental function of the unconscious mind is to

work on materializing its database.

The irony is, some people embed faulty and dis-empowering instructions in their bio-hard-drive and then they get frustrated, if not mad, when their body follows those instructions. These people incessantly re-enforce a *"Cannot"* attitude in their mind, yet expect a *"Can"* performance. They are the ones that insist on repeating their actions every day and expect different results. When they don't, they curse anything and everything except themselves. What happens when they do so? They'll deprive themselves from learning to make better decisions simply because they mastered the de-activation of their *"Failure Mechanism"*, right?

Therefore, if you are not happy with any aspect of your life, please examine what you stored in your un-conscious mind to that regard because your behaviour will always be, and with no exception, consistent with what you already have in there.

Here is what Dr. Denis Waitley had to say:

"What the mind dwells upon, the body acts upon".

Stated differently by Dr. Maxwell Maltz, the author of Psycho-Cybernetics, he quotes:

"If you think of yourself as a duckling, you're going to talk like a duckling and you're going to walk like a duckling".

That is, don't expect any different results from what *you* instilled in your bio-hard-drive. It will always be "Input = Output" and ..."Cause & Effect".

So, the unconscious mind will always say to the conscious mind, "Yes Master and let me help you live it", and then give instructions to your nervous system to act accordingly, which also indicates that there is total harmony and congruency between body & mind and one will always follow the other. That is to say, when you're in a good mood, it's impossible for your body to show otherwise, and the opposite is also true.

The rule is:

Your body posture will always be in synch with your mood and your mood will always mirror your body posture.

Fix one and you'll fix the other, automatically. If you are not in a good mood, for example, just straighten your body-posture to as if you are in a good mood and you'll snap out of it in a couple of minutes! Guaranteed! Why? Because our nervous system is a two-way street and its primary function is to keep our body and mind in unison. We are wired that way, might as well take advantage of this connection.

So can you see how everything is linked together starting from that one thought, leading to self-programming, to behaviour, and outcome? Okay let's find out more about how our brain works. The 4th attribute of the unconscious mind…

4. It Manages Thousands Of Tasks.

Again, do you still remember what I said about the conscious mind in that regard? The conscious mind can only entertain one thought at a time, right? Conversely, the unconscious mind manages every single cell and organ in our body 24-7-365 days a year, as well as it takes instructions from the conscious mind, and all at once. Let me give you an example: Did it ever occur to you that all you remember from a trip is putting your key in the ignition switch, starting your engine, and the next thing you remember is parking your car somewhere? Did you ever have such an experience? If you drive, then I am pretty sure that you did! Now who was driving your car all of that time? Was it your conscious mind, or your unconscious mind? Yes, your un-conscious mind was handling all aspects of your driving experience while you were consciously preoccupied. You were talking either to yourself or to someone else, right?

In psychology, they call this experience as being in a

"Dissociated Trance". When you are in this kind of trance you become consciously separated from what you are doing and you rely on your unconscious mind to handle the job for you.

Nearly 95% of our daily activities are done while we are in this kind of trance. That is, 95% of our daily activities are done while we are on "Auto-pilot", or robotic mode, if you will. Is being in this state of mind a good thing, or a bad thing? Well, it all depends on what you have saved on your bio-hard-drive. If you instilled "success" programs in there and you go on autopilot, then this is great because your unconscious mind will continuously execute successful behaviours and you'll reap its rewards. We all strive to reach this height. We all want successful behaviours to be the dominant factor in our lives. Conversely, if you have a couple of bad programs in there and you go on autopilot, your behaviour and outcomes will be rather disappointing.

Now, do you know what the common name to these programs is? These programs are called our *"Habits"* and we'll talk about the role they play in our lives and their relationship to our success very soon. Let's finish the seven attributes first. The 5th attribute of the unconscious mind…

5. Can Detect Super Fast Images

An experiment was conducted a few years ago. They brought in twenty volunteers suffering from snake-phobias, wired them to check their heart-rate, blood-pressure, and galvanic-skin-response (*perspiration*) and then put each one of them in front of a computer monitor. They told them that they'd show them a series of twenty-five pictures. Each picture would appear on the screen for three seconds and two of these pictures, let's say #5 and #15, for example, would be of snakes.

When those pictures came up on the screen, the scientists closely watched their equipment to see if there was any kind of reaction such as a change in the volunteer's heart rate, blood pressure, and perspiration. When the volunteers saw these pictures, there was no reaction. Why? Because they consciously knew that they were just looking at pictures. There was nothing to fear from a picture.

What the scientists did not tell those volunteers is that they would also flash on the computer screen two more pictures of snakes for a period of 40/1000th of a second (*four milliseconds*). Now since the conscious mind functions much slower than the unconscious mind, the volunteers couldn't consciously detect the fast moving images on their monitors and, as such, they were not even aware that they saw those two fast moving pictures.

When they were asked right after the experiment if they saw any other pictures of snakes they all confirmed that they only saw two pictures, 5 and 15. Scientists' equipment, however, indicated a different story. When the two fast moving pictures of the snakes were flashed on the screen, every volunteer's body reacted exactly as if they saw a real snake. Okay, what is the implication of this? Our programming and re-programming is done the same way.

This is how advanced marketers apply sub-liminal stimulation on the masses! Slipping information under our mental radar without being *aware* of it, that is. "Liminal" means, *"Awareness Threshold"*. *Sub*-liminal therefore is anything that is below and beyond our conscious mind's threshold. Some of the ads we see, whether on TV, in magazines, or bill-boards mostly contain sub-liminal messages that we are not aware of and that's where *emotion* and *association* variables greatly influence our programming. Is it legal? Contrary to public belief, subliminal advertising is legal. If you want to know more about this subject you can start with a good book called *"The Secret Sales Pitch"* by August Bullock. It's about subliminal advertising and how the media manipulates our unconscious mind to their agent's exclusive advantage. Well, welcome to *"Brain Control Age"*! It's here and happening to us everyday.

Another concept that is exploiting neuro-science is called *"Neuro-marketing"*. When companies conduct a neuro-marketing research they put volunteers in an fMRI scanner. In case you don't know the difference between MRI and f-MRI scanners, MRI (*Magnetic Resonance Imaging*) scans the *physical* structure of the brain. f-MRI, on the other hand, scans the *functions* of the brain. While in the scanner, they show the volunteer a series of pictures about products they intend to manufacture to see what triggers excitement in people's brains, what could be associated with specific demographics, and what consumers cannot resist. Is this concept only used in marketing? How about politics and selling, to name a few. They now know how certain words influence our decisions and they use them to make us agree to whatever they want to sell, be it politics or products. Mind you, there is no intimidation involved in this process. It's only about going into our brain, see what we like, and then exploit it to their advantage. It's also about what we don't like and then either try to avoid it or wittingly go around it. Mix this with hypnosis and we become nothing but living robots.

But what else is this snake phobia experiment telling us about the unconscious mind? Let's go to attribute #6 to find out.

6. Cannot Distinguish Between: Truth/Lie, Good/Bad, Real/Imagined Events

Two separate experiments were conducted to unravel the secrets of the unconscious mind. The first was done in Austria where they took a medical student, put him in a wheel chair, then took him on a tour throughout the walkways of the hospital and asked him to remember his tour as much as he could. Right after, they put him into a PET-Scan and then asked him to close his eyes and visualize his trip throughout the hospital. To the doctors' amazement at the time, the PET scan showed that his *"Primary Visual Cortex"*, which controls the sight function, was active as if the student was really looking and experiencing his trip throughout the walkways of the hospital.

The second experiment was conducted by the Cleveland Clinic Foundation. They asked thirty young adults to *visualize* moving their little finger muscle as strongly as they could and make the exercise as real as possible, without moving their fingers. The duration of experiment was for twelve weeks, five minutes a day, five days per week. Right after, they compared the results to another group that only did a physical exercise. The group that did the mental exercise increased their little finger muscles by 35%, just by visualizing the exercise, and that was almost identical to the physical group.

Okay, what does all of this mean? Obviously, it means that our unconscious mind cannot tell the difference between real and imagined experiences. It also means that our *"Synthetic Experience"* has the same effect on our brain and behaviour as much as, if not more than, our *"Actual Experience"*. Further, it also means that our unconscious mind stores all information received as *real* and consequently gives instructions to our nervous system to function as such.

Did you ever watch a movie and cried? Why did you cry although you are fully aware that it's just a movie? You cried, or started biting your fingernails, because in order for you to enjoy the movie, you consciously suspended your judgment and since your unconscious mind cannot tell the difference between real and imagined experiences...you cry. That is why we react to movies the way we do!

This is an extremely powerful concept that has a tremendous impact on our lives. It can *empower* us, such as when we deliberately do a visualization session on a regular basis, or it can *dis-empower* us, such as when we inadvertently play negatively structured visualization sessions. We'll talk more about the power and impact of visualization when we get to "Your Success Recipe" in Part Two. For now let's talk about the 7th attribute of the unconscious mind.

7. It Does Not Respond To Negative Feedback

Okay, what do I mean by that? There is a concept that I call *"The Law Of Negative Focus"* and it goes like this:

When we focus our mind on what we do not want, subconsciously, we remain bound by that undesired

thought or idea.

Said differently, when you consciously think of what you do not want to happen, such as repeating to yourself something like:

- *"I don't want to be fat"*
- *"I don't want to be unemployed"*
- *"I don't want to be miserable"*
- *"I don't want to be in debt"*
- *"I don't want to be late"*

Unconsciously, you'll keep on moving toward achieving that undesired wish. If I say to you *"Don't think of an apple!"* What did you think of first? An "apple", then you tried not to think of an apple, right? Again, it's just the way our brain works!

The conscious mind fully understands the message as spoken. The unconscious mind, however, does not understand negative requests such as "Don't" or "Not to", and as such it will automatically work on the rest of the sentence. Thus, instead of reacting on *"Do not think of an apple"*, it responds to *"think of an apple"*, which is a *command* to the unconscious mind to act upon.

Another classic example of this law is when we say to our children something like, *"Don't spill the milk"*. What do they do a minute later? They...*spill the milk*. Having said that, here's how you can scare off your customers. Just say, *"Don't worry* Mr. Customer. Everything will be just fine!"*, or say something like, *"Don't worry!* It will be delivered on time". What will happen when you say something like this? You'll inadvertently direct their mind to what you don't want them to think of...and "boom"! They become worried because of what you just said, and without even knowing why. So how do we fix this, or say it right, at least? Follow this rule:

Focus your mind on what you want rather than on what you do not want!

Just ask yourself this question: What do I want instead? By doing so, you switch your focus to what you want rather than to what you don't want. Thus, instead of saying:

- "Don't spill the milk". You can say something like, "*Pay attention* to your cup" or "*Be careful*"
- "Don't worry". You might say, "*I assure you*"
- "Don't panic". Say, "*Remain calm*"
- "I don't want to be fat". Say, "*I want to be* slim"
- "I don't want to be in debt". Say, "*I want to be financially independent*"

Do you see the difference? This is one important way to streamline some of our brain's functions and make it more efficient, productive, and powerful. This is how we can make our brain work for us rather than against us. This is how we build stepping-stones to our success rather than barriers to our progress. Now let's move on to the next chapter to learn more.

"Before an egg can grow into a chicken,
it must first totally cease to be an egg.
Each thing must lose its original identity
before it can be something else"

–Perle Epstein

Chapter 4

Anatomy Of Choice

"Being brought to life was not your choice, what you make of it is your choice!" –Saleem Bidaoui

Every conscious thought you think of is a choice. At any moment in time you can choose what to focus on, and what not to focus on, what to think of, and what not to think of, what to listen to, and what not listen to, what to look at, and what not to look at, and so on. Unlike animals, we've been privileged with the ability to choose.

Whatever you choose to focus on, however, you can also choose to label it as positive, or negative. This is also a choice. Any thought, situation, or event you may encounter, you have the choice to give it a positive or negative meaning.

In summary then, our conscious thoughts are nothing but choices we make every single minute of our lives and the meaning we give to these thoughts is also a choice! Believe it or not, what you *choose* to focus on and the *meaning* you give to your choices on a daily basis is one fundamental approach to controlling the electro-chemical process in your brain. Anything you can think of, including your happiness, health, success, and destiny, is entirely dependent on the choices you make every day. Suffice it to say, you *choose* what to bring into your life.

Negative thoughts and choices will literally trigger the release of toxic chemicals that will be carried through your blood stream and to every single cell in your body. Done repeatedly, these choices will ruin your mood, affect your decisions, overall health, relationships, and the quality of your life as well. Negative thoughts create nothing but a trail of invisible destruction starting from the inside out. Unfortunately, in many cases we don't even notice it happening until it's too late.

Be careful with your daily choices because that's where your future begins.

Conversely, positive thoughts will trigger the release of chemicals that will promote pleasure and tranquility in the brain. These chemicals will also be carried through your blood stream and to every single cell in your body. There is ample medical evidence to support the fact that positive choices will actually boost your immune system and brainpower leading to better decisions, mood, health, happiness, relationships, and longer life.

All said and done, each conscious thought is a choice, and each choice has a physical effect on all aspects of your life. Each thought you choose to think of will act as throwing a pebble in the middle of a still pond. It will reverberate and create a ripple effect starting from your brain and all the way down to your toes.

Now let's take our choices one-step further. If we can only think of one thing at a time and we choose to think of what makes us sad or mad, what do we automatically eliminate from our mind at the same time? We eliminate what makes us happy or calm, right? How do we feel as a result? Obviously, we will feel sad, or mad.

That is to say, each thought you choose to think of will set the stage to how you're going to feel right after. As such, can we say that happiness, or misery, is a choice? You bet we can! All we have to do at any moment in time is to focus on one of these and we'll automatically eliminate the other then instantly live and feel the impact of our choices. Will this also affect our success, happiness, and the overall quality of our life? I am sure you'll agree with me that we "choose" to win or lose, to be happy or miserable, don't we?

Your whole life is the by-product of the choices you make... or don't make.

Whether to attend school or not to attend school is a choice. To advance in life or stay where you are right now is a choice. To pay now and play later is a choice. To play now and pay later is also a choice. Just remember that the choices you made yesterday got you to where you are today. Whether you like it or not, the choices you make *today* will define your tomorrow. My question to you is this: What kind of tomorrow do you want? *It is your choice!*

The "Thought Switch" Technique

There are times, however, when we suddenly find our-selves in the middle of a negative thought, and like a whirlpool, we find it extremely hard to pull out of it at that moment. Have you ever had such an experience? A time when you felt you were ruminating a negative thought and got angrier and angrier rather than calming down? So what do you do in this case?

In 1997, just a couple of months before I left Canada to live overseas, an infomercial went on TV for a self-development program. I liked what the program was about so I picked up the phone and ordered it. My eldest daughter looked at me and said, "Oh no! You fell for that Dad?" Well, *that* changed my entire life and put me on a totally different path.

In 1999, while I was still living overseas, I went through the worst period of my life. I can easily say that it was the year I graduated from the "Hard-Knocks University". That Year, I was in the middle of total chaos, confusion, financial disaster, and tremendous pressure from everyone around me, including my parents.

To give you an example of how bad it was, during that period my children showed signs of malnutrition and my wife didn't know what to cook for the next day simply because we had no money. Not to mention the emotional roller-coaster that came as a bonus. You see, when you have no one to care for, you really don't care whether you eat for one day or not. However, when you have a family that you love and care about yet don't know what to feed them for lunch the next day, it is a nerve-racking experience that can drain your energy very quickly.

I have a cousin who sympathized with us and felt the distress we were experiencing. He tried to help in any way he could at a time when most people we knew just abandoned us. One day as we were chatting, he looked at me and said, "How can you handle all of this pressure? If I were you I would've committed suicide" That was comforting, wasn't it? Actually, he was stunned by how cool, calm, and collected I was during that category-10 hurricane I went through that year. Do you still remember the guy who used to flip on trivial things? Now he's cool, calm and collected at the peak of adversity! How did I manage to pull that off?

Three things helped me keep my sanity during that time:

1. The power of faith.
2. Emotionally, it was the unconditional love and support I received, and still receive from my beloved wife.
3. Mentally though, it was due to a technique I learned from the program that I had purchased before leaving Canada to live overseas.

One of the most powerful techniques that I've ever learned and that made a big, big, big, difference in my life was what I call, *"The Thought Switch Technique"*, and it goes like this:

Whenever your brain drives you into a negative territory, and it will, stop it immediately, and change your focus to something better. You have the choice!

Whenever one of those destructive thoughts attempted to dominate my focus I used to say, "detach, detach...", and I immediately snapped out of it. That's how I managed to alleviate that overwhelming pressure.

Did I master this technique overnight? No, of course not! I *trained* myself to control this process and eventually I did. Nowadays I don't have to say "detach", "dis-engage", "stop", or "cancel" anymore. Anytime I find myself getting sucked into something negative or un-productive, I just switch.

You too can train yourself to become aware of your negative thoughts and then train yourself to switch. You'll gradually start controlling this empowering process and eventually master it. Trust me, getting used to applying this technique will make a big difference in your life.

One Caveat: The brain cannot sit quiet and unless you quickly fill-in the void after you switch thoughts to a positive and productive one, it will pull you back to your previous thought, especially if it happened to be an emotionally charged one.

In case you're wondering about the name of that program and the genius behind it, the program is called: *"Personal Power II."* and the master behind it is Mr. Anthony Robbins, of course. I call him "The mentor that I've never met".

The Two Of You

Do you believe me if I say there are two of you? There is! From the outside, you are only one. From the inside, however, there's "You", and there's "Yourself", and "You" always talk to…"Yourself", right? Don't worry we all do! Now, is "self-talk" a conscious, or an unconscious activity? Self-talk is a conscious activity that will program your entire life and create your present, as well as your future. You are today the total sum of what *"You"* say to *"Yourself"* and we'll talk about that in further detail.

Is "daydreaming" a conscious, or an unconscious activity? Not sure! Here's a question that will jog your memory. When you drive your car and daydream at the same time, will you be consciously aware of your surrounding? No, not entirely, at least! You'll be in a totally different world. Thus, daydreaming is a conscious activity, and this is extremely important for you to know.

Now how about "listening"? Is it a conscious, or an unconscious activity? Obviously, listening is a conscious activity. Having said that, let's say you are engaged in a self-talk, daydreaming, or thinking of what to say next, and consciously you can only entertain one thought at a time. Can you listen effectively at the same time? Of course not! What's the remedy then? The remedy is to make an effort to listen actively and be non-judgmental. Now you know the first and most important key to effective listening.

In summary then, the choices we make and the quality of the conversation we conduct with ourselves on a regular basis will become a command to our unconscious mind and in turn it will attempt to bring it to life and make it real. Having said that, then it is wise to be careful with what we say to ourselves because our self-talk, repeated too often, will become a self-fulfilling prophecy.

The Sage Grandpa

Now let me rap up talking about the anatomy of choice with the following parable:

A Native-Indian boy was sitting with his grandfather on top of a hill one day enjoying the sunset and the landscape in front of them. The boy asked his grandfather, *"Grandpa, how do you describe the world today?"*

His sage grandfather looked at him and said, *"Like two wolves fighting inside of my heart. One is full of hate and anger, and the other one is full of peace and love."*

"But which one will win, grandpa?", the boy asked.

His grandfather hugged him and said, *"The one I feed will win"*. *"The one I feed will win"*.

Needless to say, the thoughts we engage ourselves in and feed to our unconscious mind will win the day, and it's an absolute choice!

Chapter 5

Anatomy Of Habits

"Success is a mental exercise...so is failure."
—Saleem Bidaoui

A habit is the automatic trigger of a specific behaviour. Habits are programs created by our brain to free the limited capacity of the conscious mind. Habits alleviate the pressure of having to deal with every single task on a conscious level starting from scratch every time we need to repeat that task. Thus, it is our habits that make life much easier for us. Just imagine we have to go through the same cycle of learning every time we have to do something like riding a bike. Life would be unbearable, not to mention the time wasted starting all over again.

To understand how habits form and how they affect every aspect of our lives, however, let's examine how they develop in babies since that's where it all starts. One of the first major events in a baby's life is when they first begin to walk. Here's what happens in their brain as they attempt to achieve that goal. The first time a baby tries to walk, tens of millions of neurons are assigned to that specific task of walking. Now, with each consecutive attempt, their *"Failure Mechanism"* kicks-in, analyzes the *"Feedback"* coming from their body through their nervous system, and then will instruct the relevant portion of the brain that is associated with that task to take corrective action. With each consecutive attempt to walk, the brain will order the neurons that are not performing well to slowdown until they eventually stop firing. The neurons that are doing better, on the other hand, are instructed to become more active and strengthen their firing. Right after, these neurons consolidate to form a network, or a program, for that specific task. This process is repeated countless number of times until all of the mediocre neurons are eliminated and good performing neurons prevail. That's how the baby develops his/her walking skills.

Another good example is when a baby first tries to eat by him/ herself. When they first attempt to do so, does the spoon go straight to their mouth? No, of course not! The first few hundred trials the spoon will normally go to the general area of the mouth and after numerous attempts they slowly, but surely, start coordinating their moves and voila! Now they have a well-coordinated program that we call a HABIT!

Neurologically speaking though, a thought, or the will to execute an action, starts in the conscious mind which is the frontal part of the brain. With each extra attempt, that thought starts moving more and more toward the bottom of the brain to the cerebellum area. As you remember, the cerebellum handles the automatic part of our brain. Now listen to this: It's only when a thought or action, reaches this part of the brain that a habit is formed. What does that mean? First, it means that we cannot achieve the simplest task, such as bringing a cup to our mouth, without forming a habit first. Secondly, it means that anything you want to be good at and master, you have to keep on working on it until it reaches that autopilot portion of your brain. Research shows that it takes at least three weeks of repeated action for that thought to get there. Some thoughts or actions may take much longer. So be patient!

In summary, any unconscious activity we can perform with ease is due to this process and anything we can do while we are on "auto-pilot" is due to a readily formed habit.

We are not born with the skill to do anything until we form a habit first.

It's only by forming a habit that we succeed. That is, we cannot eat, drink, walk, ride a bike, drive a car, play tennis, or anything else without forming a habit first.

Habits are our genetic roadmap to success

Are our habits confined to movement and daily activities? Habits permeate every aspect of our lives and they go way beyond mere activities. Listening, positive and negative attitude, self-talk, thinking, enthusiasm, self-confidence, the vocabulary we use every day, and the questions we ask ourselves and to others, to name a few, are all habitual. Almost 95% of what we do every single day is habitual.

Now if 95% of what we do on a regular basis is habitual and robotic, then suffice it to say that 95% of our success is directly attributed to the *quality of habits,* we develop and work with every day. In other words, the quality of our lives is about the quality of our habits and this is another major difference between successful and unsuccessful people. Successful people develop successful habits such as positive attitude and perseverance. Un-successful people on the other hand develop unsuccessful habits such as incompetence, procrastination, and giving up too quick too soon.

Successful people make a habit of what unsuccessful people don't like, or dare, to do.

Here's what Confucius had to say about habits:

"The nature of man is always the same; it is their habits that separate them".

All in all, if you are looking for different kinds of results in your life, then you need to develop different kinds of habits! There is no other way around it!

Inception of Success

Let's take a closer look at the process of forming habits. What does this process start with? It all starts with a specific "Goal". A goal to walk, to eat, to play, to become a golfer, a lawyer, a doctor, etc. These are all goals. Now let's go back to the baby example for a minute. Babies are the best example by the way because they start from zero. Right after a baby sets on a goal such as to eat by themselves or walk on their own, he/she automatically proceeds to what? They proceed to taking "Action", right? Now do they succeed on their first trial? No, of course not! So, what do they encounter on their way to achieve their desired goal? Obviously, they encounter countless number of "Errors"…and a couple of bumps on the head as a bonus. Do they get discouraged and give up as a result? We know better that they don't! They fearlessly and relentlessly keep on repeating the same cycle of trial and error "Until". Until what? Until they develop the "Skill" that will help them achieve their goal. That's why children don't take "No" for an answer, by the way! They get conditioned early in life that if they insist and persist on something, eventually, they're going to get it. Un-fortunately, some people reverse this mindset as they grow older and form the habit of quitting too soon. Just one bump on the head and they throw-in the towel.

Now think about it. As simple as it is to walk or as sophisticated as flying the space shuttle, we still have to follow exactly the same process of forming a habit first in order to succeed, don't we? That is to say, nobody ever did anything perfectly well with no previous or relevant experience. Having said that, then whatever you wish to succeed in, you have to take your time to form the habit of doing it well, first. This is your only straight path and shortest way to success, and there's no other way around it. Habits are our genetic roadmap to success, and success is merely a collection of successful habits.

Expressed eloquently by Greek Philosopher Aristotle 2300 years ago, he said,

"We are what we repeatedly do. Excellence then is not an act, but a Habit".

Read that again! Excellence is a *habit*. Success is a habit. Habits are another evidence that we are equipped and born ready to succeed. We succeeded in forming every habit we have so far, and every habit we have is a proof of our successes. Your whole life, however, is about the sort of habits you succeeded in forming so far.

Four Steps to Excellence

In summary then, the process of forming a habit and excellence involves four steps:

1. **Select a Specific Goal**
   Be it to play golf, or to become a millionaire, success starts with the intention and a clear vision of what you want to achieve. If you don't know what you want to be or do in life, that's exactly what you're going to get, and you'll hit it with unparalleled precision. To get what you want, on the other hand, you must know exactly what you want and your loyal servant will automatically work on bringing it to reality.

2. **Take Action Immediately**
   That is, invest your energy in moving toward what you really want in life. Automatically take action toward achieving your goals because the more you procrastinate and contemplate, the more you'll be late in getting to what you want.

3. **Accept Your Mistakes**
   This is the only way to grow. Give an opportunity to your *"Failure Mechanism"* to kick-in and help you take corrective action. Accept the fact that your mistakes are your stepping-stones to your success. That's where successful habits start.

4. **Keep On Going *Until***
   Whether you want to be a skier or a public speaker, keep on doing it until you master it. There's no better way to achieve

excellence. Never give up too quickly and then say it doesn't work. I spent twenty years in this vicious cycle not knowing why things didn't work for me. I used to try something for a while and if it didn't work, I abandoned it and started something else, and then something else, in a never-ending cycle. No wonder nothing worked in my life for a while!

To Learn & Unlearn

Keep in mind that success cannot be cooked in a micro-wave oven. It takes ten long years of study, hard work, and practice to earn the enviable title of a "Doctor". There are no shortcuts except in the heads of unsuccessful people, and life always proves them wrong. You must follow the Four Steps to Excellence! Just remove any of these steps and success is almost, if not surely, impossible!

Statistically speaking, nearly 90% of people who attend seminars, for example, don't really benefit from the programs they attend simply because they don't know about this principle. They attend a seminar and learn something that could enhance, or maybe change the entire course of their lives, yet don't follow up and persevere to reach that level of excellence. A couple of weeks later and that seminar is just a good memory. Not knowing that they must first form the habit of what they just learned in order to reap the rewards of their investment. Now you know!

Okay, so far we discussed how neurologically habits form in the brain and their direct link to permanent success. Now here's a scientific fact and a profound rule that will bring relief to those who really want to change:

Whatever we learn, we can unlearn!

That is to say, any habit you may have formed in the past and find it limiting or disempowering, you can get rid of it and replace it with a better one. No excuses!

Thus, and this is painful to admit by some people, when someone says "I cannot change" or "I was born that way", all they are saying is, "I don't want to change and I like myself this way". Well, that's their choice.

As for you, any habit you have and find it self-defeating or dis-empowering, you can replace it with an empowering one. How? In exactly the same way you formed the old one. That's how! Just follow the "Four Steps to Excellence" and your unconscious mind will make sure that you get there. You are the "rider" and you know perfectly well how to control your "horse" from now on. Just stay on the path long enough to form the habit of what you want and your life will be heading in a new direction.

The Three Controllers

Okay, now let's say you are interested in sales as a career and you go and attend professional workshops and then follow through. Will this guarantee that you'll be highly successful in your endeavour? Well, training and following through are crucial to success and will definitely guide you in the right direction. However, it will not guarantee a high level of success because everything we do is subject to a couple of "controllers" that will also influence the quality of our decisions, habits, and life in general. These controllers shape our preferences and steer us in one direction or the other.

Take two salespeople, for example. Both have the same qualifications, work for the same company, attended the same training, receive same input, put in same hours, and face the same environment every day, yet one produces totally different results from the other. This is the case in every profession, industry, and company. Why is it like that? It is mainly due to three gatekeepers that will either help you fly high or spend your life on the tarmac of mediocrity and stagnation. So let's go to the next chapter and find out about the first of these controllers.

"In life, you don't get what you want, you get what you are"

– Les Brown

Chapter 6

Anatomy Of
Beliefs

"You can never be more than what you think you can"
–Saleem Bidaoui

One of the most powerful things that influence the direction of our lives is our *"Belief System"*. Our beliefs are the compass of our preferences and behaviour. They define for us what is pleasure and pain, what we can or cannot do, good and bad, what to accept or reject, love or hate, what to read, wear, eat, and so on. Some of our beliefs are true, while others only exist in our minds. Valid or invalid, beliefs shape our reality as well as set the boundaries of our potential.

In the last century or so racing horses improved their performance by an average of 3% due to enhanced training techniques and proper dieting. Human beings, on the other hand, improved their performance by an average of 40% within the same period. Why? Simply because human beings *believe* they can and, as such, they do! Equipped with beliefs, humans have tools that can lift them to eternity, or drag them on a straight path to extinction. Animals don't have this kind of luxury.

Our "Belief System" is the first checkpoint that will define our attitude and altitude in any endeavour. Our beliefs can provide us with the thrust we need to soar with eagles, and have the doors of possibility wide open, or they can hold us back by erecting mental barriers between us and the success we seek.

Here are some of the beliefs that will direct your brain as well as everything else in your life towards failure:
- *"I hate myself"*
- *"I am not worthy of success"*
- *"I am too old, too short, too white, too dark, etc."*
- *"I'll be happy when I succeed"*
- *"Opportunity only knocks once"*
- *"My life is a disaster waiting to happen"*
- *"I can never be on time"*
- *"I hate my job"*
- *"Life stinks!"*

Do these statements look familiar to you? Do you know someone who keeps on repeating some of these dis-empowering statements? I am sure you do! No statement is more powerful and destructive, however, than the first one. When someone keeps on saying, *"I hate myself"*, it simply means they're not worth achieving anything. In such a case, will their brain help them succeed? Of course not!

Just imagine someone keeps on saying to themselves day in and day out something like, *"I am not that smart"*. How will their unconscious mind respond to such a repetitive input? "Yes Master and let me help you live it". As such, their unconscious mind will re-enforce those beliefs by making sure they perform accordingly. Now is it true that these people are not smart? Highly unlikely!

As you can see, some people set themselves up on a straight path to failure and based on this they'll create the evidence that will support their erroneous beliefs of incompetence. That's why some people have more faith in winning the lottery than in their own ability to create success, financial independence, and happiness in their lives. They are ready, capable, and well equipped for success, yet held back by their own *"Mental Brakes"*. They are just like a car with a twelve cylinders engine, yet their parking (mental) brake is applied. So powerful, yet it can go nowhere! Such beliefs limit our true potential while in reality they are nothing but illusions that some people voluntarily adhere to.

Scientifically speaking though, you have an invaluable and potent asset between your ears that can get you anything you want in life...*only if you believe in it*. Think of those who achieved something significant in their lives. Did they get there because they believed they *can*, or believed they *can't* and it just happened to them? You know the answer, don't you? Thus,

Believe and you'll achieve!

Believe in your capacity to reach higher grounds, sustain success, good health, and happiness, and you will achieve that. Conversely, believe that you are nothing but a failure and you'll achieve it with a flare. I've done it for a while and I was so successful at it. Believe in sickness and misery and your loyal servant will get you there. Believe that you cannot be financially independent and your wish will come true. Believe that you are doomed to poverty, and you'll join the club. But don't think this club's membership is cheap or free! The poverty club membership is extremely expensive but most impoverished (by choice) members don't know that. Think about it. To join this club you have to deny your *true potential* and all of the money you could accumulate as a result. Expensive, isn't it?

Here's a fundamental question that I want you to think of, seriously: If you already have the potential to have a decent job or business and *can* accumulate one, five, ten million, or a billion dollars during your lifetime, how much would you've given-up just to join this club?

The irony is that this club has more members than any other club on earth. What's so sad about the whole thing is that over half of its members join by choice. Another important question in here is the following: Are you currently a member of this club? If you are, but don't like their privileges and "Customer Service" any more, then it's time to consider the alternatives offered to you in this book. Believe and you will achieve! It is that simple!

Believe in what you want to see in your life and you will see it. That's what your brain does best and it all starts with that *one thought* we talked about. Keep your focus on something rewarding, positive, and productive, and your unconscious mind will say, "Yes Master and let me help you live it". Not only that, but by doing so you'll instantly eliminate all counter-productive thoughts from your mind. Focus your thoughts strictly on success and you'll automatically eliminate failure from your life. Focus it on happiness and you'll automatically eliminate misery and pain. Focus it on wealth and you'll eliminate poverty from your mind…and your life as well.

In case you're wondering about my definition of poverty verses financial independence, here's how I discriminate between the two: If one can pay for a major surgery from his/her own pocket, in case they urgently need it, then I consider them as financially independent. Having an insurance policy as an alternative does not mean that it's okay. Remember, if you have a life policy for a million dollars it doesn't mean that you are a millionaire. Anything less than what I just mentioned simply means you are currently a member of the poverty club and need to seriously assess your membership privileges, which I think are closer to none!

Law of Inertia Revisited

For things to change in your life you must believe that you can do so and have the courage to take the first step out of your current position. Nothing will change in your life until you take the first step to change it. This is what the "Law of Inertia" is all about. The more you think about how this Law applies to you, the more you're going to see how you can achieve different results in your life.

The Law of Inertia states that,

"Every object persists in its state of rest…or uniform motion unless it is compelled to change that state by forces impressed on it".

Said differently, your life will stay the way it is until you take the initiative and put the effort to change the status quo. Nothing will change by itself. Thus don't wait!

Bottom line: Believe in your capacity to change and you will. Believe that you can achieve whatever you want and you will. Choose your goals wisely and focus your thoughts on the kind of life that you deserve and your unconscious mind will help you bring it to reality. It's that one thought and that one thought is merely what you believe. What you believed in yesterday created your present and what you believe in today will create your tomorrow. Your beliefs will come to life, be it positive or negative. Hence, your life is your choice and you know better by now how to make it more successful!

The Dis-Oriented Diver

Do you know what happens to a diver when they get disoriented under water? I used to be a skin-diver. That is, I used to dive wearing fins and mask but no oxygen tank. Just go a few meters underwater to enjoy the scenery or examine something and then come up again.

On a couple of occasions, I had the opportunity to sit down and chat with an amateur, but experienced, diver. He used to tell me stories about the pleasures and perils of diving. How to avoid a shark attack, how to empty the water from your mask while underwater, and among other things he told me how an inexperienced diver without a pressure suit may get disoriented due to pressure change at a certain depth. He said, when this happens, the diver will become disoriented and they will lose their sense of direction. They'll start diving deeper and deeper thinking that they're heading up to the surface. If they are alone and nobody notices where they're going, it becomes a death sentence because they'll exhaust their oxygen supply while they are still going in the wrong direction.

I think this is a good analogy to *"Limiting Beliefs"* because they induce the same kind of illusion and unless we realize them as such, those beliefs will exhaust life itself while we are still going in the opposite direction of our "True Potential".

Unfortunately, most people take limiting beliefs passively, feed them to their unconscious mind, and then wonder why they can't get anywhere in life. They don't realize that in most cases those beliefs were based on one or two screw-ups and they voluntarily labelled them as the rule rather than the exception. Such people forget all of their successes in life, big or small, and focus on a couple of mishaps, and then call them the norm not realizing that when repeated this mindset will become their reality and they'll get caught in a vicious circle by creating the evidence that will support those beliefs. That's how some people create the illusion of ineptitude, lack of confidence, and a sense of failure, which is enough to destroy their ambition and get them going in the wrong direction of life.

Perception & Beliefs

Does our perception, which is based on our beliefs, affect our behaviour and outcome? Listen carefully to this:

In most cases, the events or situations we encounter are neutral and we label them according to our beliefs.

Here is an example of what I mean: Two passengers sitting in an airplane and waiting for takeoff. They're both in exactly the same situation, environment, event, reality, or whatever you want to call it. Is there anything wrong with this situation? No, of course not! It is neutral. Nothing is scary or exciting about it, yet one of them is clenching the armrest out of fear, while the other one is thrilled about the whole thing.

What's different about those two passengers? The only difference between them is how each one of them labelled the situation at hand. One thought of it as a terrible experience in progress and as such he became terrified about the whole event, while the other one believed that it's going to be exhilarating and as such he became excited about this trip.

Two people facing the same situation, yet each person has a different label for it. "Events are neutral and *we* label them". Now with the person who became terrified, what kind of trip do you think he had? A nerve racking and a lousy one, right? The point is, when someone "believes" that his or her trip is going to be terrible, in essence, they eliminate the pleasure of that trip from their mind and they set themselves up for a terrible experience. Well, isn't that what some of us do every single day of our lives? When someone believes that he or she's an unhappy or a lousy person, salesperson, entrepreneur, manager, doctor, spouse, or whatever, they set-up themselves for what?

They will simply prep their nervous system to act accordingly. As such, what kind of trip do you think they'll have throughout their lives and careers? A rather disappointing one! Most importantly, what kind of chemicals will their brain secrete in this case? Anything but pleasure hormones, I guess! Can you see the link and implications of this kind of thinking on our lives?

In summary, we consciously choose our beliefs and our beliefs set the stage to what comes after in our lives. In other words:

We become what we believe!

Therefore, if something is not working well in your life, please examine your beliefs before attempting to fix that thing. You can attend numerous seminars and read hundreds of books about how to become happy, healthy, and wealthy. You can apply what you've learned, but if you have limiting beliefs in that area, you're not going to achieve permanent results and you'll go back to your comfort zone in no time.

Dis-empowering Limiting Beliefs

So how can you get rid of your dis-empowering beliefs? Two effective and powerful techniques that will help you achieve that:

1. Change Your Perspective

Here's one of my favourite quotes by Dr. Wayne Dyer,

"Change the way you look at things and the things you look at will change."

That is to say, change the meaning of how you look at something and you'll get different results. Just label any situation differently from what you used to label it before and you'll have different results with respect to that issue. Look at the positive aspect of a situation and your whole perspective will change. When someone cuts you off on the highway, for example, look at it as if they have an emergency rather than they are ignorant, arrogant, or just want to tick you off. Try this technique and you'll see, and feel, the difference it makes in your life!

You might experience some reluctance in the beginning but I assure you when you do it for the first time you'll experience a sense of joy and achievement. Most importantly, you'll feel that you are in control of your life. You'll feel that you have the power to change anything from now on. It's a nice feeling! Just give a different meaning to any belief that is dis-empowering you and you'll see yourself in a new world.

2. Challenge Your Disempowering Beliefs

Another remedy to get rid of your limiting beliefs is to *challenge* those beliefs. Anytime you hear something negative about yourself, whether it is internally initiated or externally dumped on you, challenge it rather than just accepting it at face value.

Whenever a disempowering belief tries to dominate your thinking and take you in the wrong direction just ask yourself if it's a valid belief. Doing this will normally bring about a change in your attitude toward that belief. Too often such a belief has no merits what so ever. Failing to achieve something, for example, does not mean that you are a "Failure", and if you failed yesterday it doesn't mean that you'll fail today or tomorrow. Failing is a means to an end. Failure on the other hand is an end, or a dead-end I should say, and there is a huge difference between these two beliefs.

Failing is an event that could have a different outcome later on, while failure is about labelling yourself with an identity that contradicts your genetic structure and I can easily say that no one is qualified for such a title. No one! Yes, you may have failed in the past, or maybe kept on failing until yesterday, but this does not mean that you are a "Failure" and you should not accept such a label from anyone, including yourself.

Challenge your limiting beliefs and your un-conscious mind will supply you with the evidence to the contrary.

Chapter 7

Anatomy Of Values

"When you insist on taking the wrong path, don't expect to find good things along the way" –Saleem Bidaoui

The second filter that has a tremendous impact on the direction of our lives is our *"Values"*. We all have an array of values that we accumulated throughout the years and which, like our beliefs, steer our preferences, decisions, and life in one direction or the other. What do successful people value, for example? Success, perseverance, financial independence, knowledge, growth, confidence, and so on, right? Do un-successful people have the same values? Not really! Just stop for a second and contemplate the difference between successful and unsuccessful people. See where each end-up in life based on their values!

Positive/Negative Values

There are two types of values: *"Positive Values"* and *"Negative Values"*. Examples of positive values include success, family, growth, achievement, etc. and examples of negative values include smoking, drinking, inaction, lying, etc. It is not these two types of values as much as it is whether we move towards or away from each that makes a difference in our lives. Nonetheless, it is the hierarchy of our values that defines our uniqueness and who we are.

Towards/Away Values

Intuitively, we are born to move towards positive values and away from negative ones. *Intellectually* however, some of us choose to do the opposite. Although achievement, for example, is the way to success, you'll find that most people shy away from making it a priority in their lives. Although smoking, by all means, is a negative value, you'll find smokers move towards it. That is to say, if someone values socializing late at night more than they value their success, for example, then we can say that they are moving toward entertainment and away from building their future and we can also presume that their life is anything but okay.

In essence, when we value success yet move away from achieving it, it is as destructive as moving toward a negative value. And unless we put our values in perspective, not much will happen in our lives.

Hierarchy Of Values

You'll find no two human beings have the same hierarchy of values and that's what makes us different. If you really want to see different results in your life, however, then it is imperative to prioritize your values and put the effort into making them a habit. We are motivated according to our values and unless we have them in good order, our life will go in the wrong direction just like the disoriented diver.

The following is a short list of thirty-three values laid down in alphabetical order:

Achievement	*Ignorance*	*Recognition*
Confidence	*Independence*	*Relationships*
Drinking	*Integrity*	*Respect*
Drugs	*Junk Food*	*Stealing*

Failure	*Knowledge*	*Security*
Family	*Laziness*	*Smoking*
Fitness	*Leisure*	*Success*
Forgiveness	*Love*	*Tardiness*
Gambling	*Lying*	*Tolerance*
Growth	*Procrastination*	*Vitality*
Health	*Power*	*Wealth*

After you read through these values please have a piece of paper and pencil ready.

Now follow these instructions:

1. Divide that sheet of paper in front of you into two columns.
2. Write the word "Positive" at the top of the first column and the word "Negative" at the top of the second column.
3. Thoroughly look at the values then write each value on that sheet of paper according to what you consider as positive or negative.
4. Now write down each value in each column based on their importance *to you* and no one else. If you think that "family", for example, is really at the top of your values list, then write "family" beside #1. If "security" is your second priority, then write "security" beside # 2, and so on.

As for your "negative values" list, #1 goes to the value you wish to avoid most. That is, if "drugs" is at the top of your negative values list, then you write it at the top and assign # 1 to that value, then #2, and keep at it until you exhaust the list. Please be honest with yourself. This list will be your *current* values' blueprint and your way of thinking up until now. By doing this exercise you'll discover a few critical things about yourself and you can change your priorities later on. As for now, prioritize them as you feel they are important to you. Not as they are important to your father, spouse, or peers, that is. You'll fix them later if you want to. Please remember that our values and their priorities change over time. What you might have as #1 today may become #4 tomorrow. So stop for a minute and prioritize your values right now.

When you are done, take a closer look at your list. Now you have a snapshot of your values and your priorities in life. Look at each value in the "Positive" column and ask yourself, "Am I really giving priority to this value or to another value instead and that's what could be creating a conflict in my life?" For example, if "Success" is your #1 value yet you spend more time on "Leisure", then there's a conflict between these two values, thus you're currently moving more towards "Leisure" than "Success" and that is affecting your life in an unproductive way. Again, it's "thought", "time", and "energy". Whatever you want to get more of, you must invest more into be it your family, success, or wealth.

Now where did you classify wealth? Did you put it with positive values, or negative values? For those who truly believe that wealth is something negative, here's the sad news:

For as long as you believe that wealth is something bad, you can never have it.

Doing so is just like dreaming of heaven, yet doing everything to qualify for hell. It's not going to happen!

Now what priority did you give to your "Health"? If it is beyond #3, then you have a problem because,

Your only true wealth is your health.

Without it you have nothing. You can have billions of dollars. But if you cannot enjoy it, how good is it to you? Not much, I guess! Thus, your first and most important asset is your health and we'll talk about that in Part Two.

Values Conflict

Now, let's say I want to have a career in sales and "Respect" is on the top of my positive values. That's absolutely fine and there is nothing wrong with that. However, if "Rejection" is also on the top of my negative values list, and to me rejection means dis-respect, will I succeed as a salesperson? I don't think so! Why? Because I have a conflict amongst my values and beliefs and I have to set the record straight in order to achieve a better outcome. Hence, unless I believe that "Rejection" mainly has nothing to do with respect and that people mainly reject my offer and not me personally, I will not succeed as a salesperson.

Now, look at the "Negative values" column and ask yourself, "Am I truly moving towards or away from any of these values?" If you claim that "smoking" is your #1 negative value, yet you smoke, you also have a problem in that area. If you find it hard to stop smoking for now, please re-assign a number that is consistent with the priority of your values. Don't worry! You can reorganize your list later on when your priorities really change.

In summary then, it's not always the value per se that influences our behaviour and outcome, but rather:

1. It's whether we move towards our positive values and away from our negative values. A good example is "health" vs. "smoking". We all designate "smoking" as a negative value yet some of us move towards smoking at the expense of our health.
2. It's how we prioritize our values in comparison to their antithesis. Again, look at "health" vs. "smoking". Which one is more important to you and which one do you really move towards or away from? Such a priority makes all the difference, doesn't it?
3. It's the congruency or conflict amongst our values that will pave the road to our success and happiness, or failure and misery. As you can see, everything counts!

Set your priorities straight to get your life straight. *It is a choice!*

"The best way to stop
a bad habit is never
to begin it"
– James C. Penny

Chapter 8

Your *Current* Identity

"You can only be what you can imagine"
–Saleem Bidaoui

Now, if you take your values and beliefs, put them in a container, close the lid and mix them really well, you'll get the third and most important filter of all. This filter will either skyrocket your success, or guarantee your failure. What do they call this filter? They call it "Self-*Image*". But what is self-image to begin with? Here's my definition to your life's silent dream-weaver:

> **Self-*image* is the internal *movie* that you produce throughout the years and play to yourself day-in and day-out. This movie is about who you *think* you are and what you can, or cannot, be or do at any given moment in time.**

Self-image is about how you see yourself in your mind's eye, which may, or may not be true at all. Saying it differently, your self-image is how you portray "you"…to "yourself". In essence, your self-image, or "Current Identity", if you will, is the creation of your "imagination" and it is done by "you" constantly repeating to "yourself" something like this: "I'm too tall or too short and ashamed of myself. I'm too beautiful and in vain or too ugly and in pain." That is to say, your self-image is about whether you think of yourself as capable, incapable, confident, insecure, successful, un-successful, healthy, overweight, smoker, golfer, smooth talker, good speaker, and so on. All of your preferences, specific style, the food you eat, the car you drive, and the clothes you wear make up your self-image as well.

When someone believes that he/she cannot be a confident speaker, for example, it's because they formed an *"image"* of a lousy speaker and played that movie over and over again until their unconscious mind stored it as *real* and then worked toward realizing it. Now, with such programming, can they go on stage and perform well? Impossible! Why? Because their loyal servant will give instructions to their nervous system to act upon their self-created database precisely as it has been stored. If their database has an image of a lousy speaker, then that's their current identity and that's exactly what they'll get. In a nutshell, that's how you become who you are today.

Good News/Bad News

To that regard though, I have "Good News" and I have Bad News". I'll start with the bad news.

- **The Bad News**

     You cannot transcend your *"Current*-Self-Image", even if you have a strong willpower!

     It's impossible to achieve better results in life beyond the image you created and *currently* maintain in your mind. Does it mean that you can never change, be better, or different? That's not what I am saying here. Listen carefully to what I just said, "You cannot transcend your *current* self-image", and by *"current* self-image" I mean the status quo. It's about what you think of yourself today and this does not include tomorrow at all.

The more you maintain the self-*image* you have right now, the more you are stuck with what you have right now.

When you currently believe that you cannot generate a certain income, for example, and you keep on saying to yourself something like *"I can never make $100,000 a year"*, or *"I can never be a successful speaker, manager, salesperson, etc."*, that's precisely what you'll manifest into your life. This is simply because that's the only image you have in your database and as such it will be the only picture that your unconscious mind can work on and bring into reality. Yes, you may have a very strong willpower and you may try many things to achieve what you want. Even if you do, it will not last for too long if your imagination is in the opposite direction of your wishes. This is because your unconscious mind can only follow and act upon the movie you created and stored in there. This is an extremely powerful concept that was first presented by a French gentleman by the name of Emile Coué, better known as, "The Father of Auto-suggestion". He said,

"When imagination and willpower are in conflict, imagination will invariably win."

To support his claim he gave a convincing example. He said, if I put a plank of wood right in front of you that is 30 centimetres wide by 30 centimetres high and 10 meters long, will you have the courage to walk on that plank of wood? Of course you do! Anyone can do that. Now if I put that same plank of wood on the top of two buildings, will you walk across? I don't know about you, but for most people the answer is a definite, "No way"! Why? Because our imagination will trigger images like, *"What if the wind threw me off balance?"*, *"What if I slipped?"*, *"What if I fainted?"*, and so on. You may not be aware of such questions, but surely they'll kick-in in circumstances like these and even if you have the willpower to take the first step on that plank of wood, your feet will involuntarily hesitate to do so by moving sideways.

Your imagination is much more powerful than your willpower and unless you work on it *first*, no *permanent* change will take place in any area of your life.

You still remember that we think in pictures, right? Based on this fact, shaping an image of what you want to achieve must always precede resorting to your willpower. Not doing so is one important reason why some people cannot achieve different results in their lives in spite of their sincere intention and desire to do so.

Let me give you another example to support this concept. Let's say that your intention is to "quit smoking" yet you have a different movie in your unconscious mind about this issue. A movie that perpetually depicts you as a smoker. That is, you constantly see yourself, in your mind's eye, taking a cigarette, lighting it, and then inhaling it with pleasure. Whether a smoker admits it or not, aware of it or not, that's what they do prior to lighting up every cigarette. That's how we think, remember? Now as such, can you quit smoking…long-term? Well, statistics show that when it comes to "kicking the habit", most people fail to achieve permanent results. Why? Simply because they only resort to using their willpower which is in opposite to how they truly label themselves. Their current-identity says, *"I am a smoker and I enjoy every puff of it"*. That's what they have in their database and that's the only thing they feel comfortable with at that time. One day, however, they wake up and say to themselves something like, *"I am going to quit smoking no matter what"*, and they are willing to bet their life on it. Who do you think will eventually win the day? Is it their current-identity, or is it their willpower? You know the answer, don't you? Definitely, it is their current-identity that will eventually prevail. Yes, they may suspend their smoking activities for a few hours, days, weeks, or maybe months, but their imagination will tease them every single day until they succumb to its dominance and go back to smoking.

Conversely, when imagination and willpower are in unison, they form a potent synergy, and this is another overlooked secret to achieving permanent success:

When your willpower and imagination are harmonious they will create miracles in your life.

That is, whatever you wish to achieve in life, keep on imagining yourself doing it then support it with your willpower by taking action in that direction. Your unconscious mind will utilize its unparalleled power to materialize it for you and bring it to life.

Everything you see around you has been brought into reality this way and now you know how to bring your dream into reality too!

Now, let's look at this concept from a different perspective. When you closely think of the word "Quitting", what comes to your mind? Something negative, right?

At a deeper level, you will find that we've been programmed since childhood to resent and resist such a word. We grew up with phrases such as, *"Quitters are losers"* and *"Winners never quit, and quitters never win"*. We grew up on the premise that we must not be quitters at any cost. Being a quitter means we give-up too quickly and don't have what it takes to win.

Therefore, the neurological resistance this word creates is engrained in the deepest level of our mind. Our deep resentment to this word, and the image it creates in our mind, will erect an invisible barrier toward giving-up smoking any time we think of quitting. The point is, even the wording of what you intend to achieve must be positive and congruent with your belief system. Words like "quitting", or "Losing", are perceived by your brain as negative concepts and as such your unconscious mind will resist working towards attaining anything that is associated with these words. The reality is, you don't want to quit smoking or lose weight. You want to be healthy and fit and the only way to achieve this goal is to keep on thinking of the future consequences of maintaining a bad habit and then resort to your willpower to *"stop"* smoking and not *"quit"* smoking. Do you see the difference? Which approach do you think is more acceptable by your unconscious mind? You're getting better at this, aren't you? Again, as you can see *everything counts*.

Okay, so far we talked about the bad news and how it's nearly impossible to achieve different results when your "*Current* Self-image" is in the opposite direction of your willpower. The main reason, being your imagination, or the movie, that *you* created for yourself and stored in your bio-hard-drive. Now let's talk about the good news.

▪ The Good News

The good news is: if you don't like what you're getting from life in general, or something specific, such as your performance, for example, you can always switch channels and watch a better movie instead. The remote control will always be in your hand and this is the beauty of our brains. How can you do that? As mentioned earlier, neuro-science has confirmed that there is no such a thing as, *"I cannot change"*, or *"I was born like that"*, or *"I am too old to change"*. In fact, your brain is changing as you read these words and you can always change for the better provided you sincerely have the desire, the intention, and the right tools to change.

You still remember that when you decide you want to achieve something, you'll eliminate all other options from your mind, and you'll start acting on that specific thought. Now think of yourself driving your favourite car. What did you see? Although I said *"think"*, you just *"imagined"* yourself driving that beautiful car, right? Normally, anything you intend to do and any action you want to take you have to imagine it first, and then you do it. Guess how you get angry, by the way? By following the same process! You have to see, or imagine, yourself as getting angry first…and then you explode! Of course, there are times when you just snap even before you think about it. That's due to a readily established habit that is linked to a certain issue (*Hot Button*). Can you get rid of such a habit? Of course you can and we talked about that.

As said earlier, smokers, for example, see them-selves in their mind's eye lighting and inhaling a cigarette before actually doing it. They associate pleasure with this act and that's what keeps them coming for more. Hence, the more they watch such a movie, the more they're going to smoke, right? How can a smoker switch channels then? They simply have to see them- selves as healthy *non-smokers*. They have to associate more and more pleasure to this bright and motivating picture, and associate more pain to their smoking movie. They have to repeat this new movie every single day until they can no longer see themselves as smokers. Only then they can use other tools, such as the patch, and enforce it with their willpower to help them get rid of such a habit.

I smoked for thirteen years and I used to light-up a cigarette the minute I woke up. Not until I got sick of seeing myself as a smoker did I become a non-smoker. I did not "quit" smoking, however. It was in June of 1983 when I looked at the pack of cigarettes I was holding in my hand and said to a friend of mine, "This is the last pack of cigarettes I am going to smoke". (*I did not throw it away thus there was no sense of loss after that*) His response was, "I want to do the same thing". Then he went further to place a bet on it. He said, "The first person who goes back to smoking must pay the other person a hundred dollars". Less than a week later he went back to smoking. Well, I did not get my hundred dollars, but won something much more important. I stayed a non-smoker ever since and today I find no prize more valuable than being healthy. How did I manage to accomplish this? This is how:

Just after one hour of dumping the disgusting habit I said to myself, "If I can go for one hour without a cigarette, then I can do the same thing for another hour" and then repeated the same thing for another hour, and another hour, until I finished my first day as a non-smoker. The next day I said to myself, "Well, if I can stay as a non-smoker for one day, then I can do the same thing for another day". Then I finished the first week as a non-smoker, then the first month, then the first year, and I haven't touched a cigarette ever since.

Now think about it! Although I didn't know it at the time, when I said to myself, "If I can stay as a non-smoker for one hour, and another hour", what was I really doing? I was creating a *new movie* in my mind as a non-smoker and then I used my willpower to follow through. My entire focus was on the pleasure of being a non-smoker; nonetheless, on the pleasure of achieving that goal. Eventually, it was *"Mission accomplished"*.

All said and done,

The *"Movie"* that you create will be the *"Reality"* that you'll activate.

Now you know more about why you are where you are and how you can get anything you want! It's no secret! Just create and maintain the image, or the movie, of what you want and stay focused like a laser beam until you get there. It's all scientific, and it's all about what *you choose* to bring into your life.

Chapter 9

Shaping Your Destiny

"We personally paint our character, life only animates it"
–Saleem Bidaoui

On average we receive about 2.4 million bits of data per minute through our senses. Out of this number, the conscious mind can only handle between three hundred to seven hundred bits of information per minute. The rest is filtered out and dealt with by the unconscious mind. Because the conscious mind has limited capacity, it selects and focuses our attention on a specific portion of that whole picture of reality that is mainly based on our own preferences. This process of selecting a specific portion of the whole picture and making it our reality is referred to in NLP (*Neuro Linguistic Programming*) as *"Mapping"*, or creating your own map of the world. No two human beings on earth have the same map, including identical twins. How we select this limited portion of information and the implication it has on the entire course of our lives is what we'll examine next.

The R.A.S.
Okay, in chapter one we talked about the brain stem, or what's known as the reptilian brain. The brain stem, just like the unconscious

97

mind, functions automatically and without any interference from us. At the junction of the brain stem and the spinal cord scientists tell us that there are a group of cells the size of the little finger known as the Reticular Activating System, or RAS, for short. This part of the brain has a lot to do with the selection of the specific bits of information we pay attention to and call reality. Our own reality, that is. Based on the three filters we talked about earlier, the RAS acts as a distribution center to those waves of data coming in either by directing them to the conscious mind as well as the unconscious mind or just the unconscious mind alone. Having said that, then the RAS plays a significant role in activating or de-activating what? Well, I just gave you the answer. It activates or de-activates the conscious mind itself. Now when the conscious mind is activated, what does this mean? It means that our attention is activated as well, right? It means we become aware of, and pay attention to, specific things in our environment.

To see the big picture of how the RAS works and why we pay attention to certain things and totally ignore other things in our environment, let's examine the RAS in further details. The RAS mainly has two major functions:

1. **Automatic Shut-down**
   The first function is to shutdown your *thinking* brain when it senses, or even perceives, any kind of danger in your environment. How does this work? Let's say you are crossing the street, for example, and a truck comes from behind and blows the horn. Do you stop or slowdown for a second and say to yourself, "Hmm, now let me think about that. Should I jump, or just keep on walking?" Do you normally do that? No, of course not! You just jump, even before you consider thinking about it, right? Another example is when you are driving and a child or an animal jumps in front of your car. Do you take the time to think whether you should hit the brakes or not? You just do it, and in a fraction of a second. No thinking is involved in this process what-so-ever. You just act by instinct. What

triggered such a quick reflex? Your RAS received information from your senses that there's a dangerous situation around you and it needs immediate attention. In a split second it jumped into overriding your thinking brain, ordering the release of adrenalin into your blood stream to increase your heart rate and make you more alert and stronger, and you instantly resort to *"Instinct Mode"*, without even thinking about it! That's what the RAS does best in times of danger and this is known as your fight/flight/freeze reflex. It is your instinctual survival mechanism, and just another example of how well equipped you are.

2. Attention Selection

The second function of the RAS is what we are interested in knowing about and which is of utmost significance to your success. It's simply about how the RAS handles your sensory input. Earlier if you still recall, I said that the only way to know anything about our external environment is through our senses. Nonetheless, without our senses we would have no experience or memory. In a nutshell then, we *learn* to see and hear. We never knew what a tree or a car looked like when we were born, did we? We accumulated that knowledge throughout the years strictly through our senses. That is to say, our senses transferred impulses, or raw data, from the environment to our brain to analyze it and make sense of it. Almost simultaneously the brain interprets what we are seeing at that moment and this information becomes what we call our reality. Your senses' job is to detect your environment and transfer that data to your brain, only. Our senses do not interpret any data and do not give it any meaning either. That's strictly done by the brain. So far so good? Great!

Now carefully think about what you are going to read next because it will change your perception as well as your life:

All sensory impulses coming in from your external environment, which are in the millions, go through the unconscious mind, thalamus, and RAS almost

simultaneously. **Since the conscious mind is very limited and cannot handle this capacity, it becomes very selective. It picks, and draws to your attention, things that are *relevant*, *important*, and *interesting* to you because it is all it can handle at one time.**

That's what makes each one of us unique, and that's why no two people will have the same map or experience.

Your Life, Your Choice

Here's a fundamental question that will test your knowledge about what you have read so far: *What do you think the conscious mind will bring to your attention in each waking moment of your life?* If you already know the answer to this question, then I would like to congratulate you from the bottom of my heart. By knowing the answer to this question you'll demonstrate that now you know how your brain really works and how to bring into your life anything you may desire, and can imagine.

Just in case you're not fully aware of its implication yet, let me explain this concept and make it 100% clear because by understanding what this means will definitely help you change your perspective as well as your destiny.

As mentioned earlier, the RAS filters and directs sensory input from your environment based on how interesting, important, or unique it is to you. Therefore, it will either make you *aware* of things that are happening in your environment, or it will de-activate your attention and make you oblivious to certain things happening around you by creating what's known in psychology as *"scotoma"*, or a blind-spot. That is to say, things will be perfectly present in front of you and around you but you won't see it or hear it because of this factor. For example, are you aware of every sound around you right now? If you said "Yes", think again! Did you ever hear about what's known as *"selective hearing"*? Women say that men have selective hearing. The reality is we all have it due to the limitations of our conscious mind.

The Relevancy Factor

Did it ever happen to you that you bought something and suddenly you noticed that everybody owns one too? Why didn't you notice it before? You didn't because it wasn't relevant to you and you weren't that interested in it before, right? Well, that's your RAS in action. But aren't you wondering about how such a selectivity develops?

Let's take the eye, for example. Why choose the eye as an example? Because at least 80% of the impulses we receive during the day come through the eye. We are almost totally dependent on our eyes to interpret the world around us. The eyes have more wiring in the brain than all of the other senses combined. That's how important our eyes are to us and I am sure you'll agree with me that a regular check up is so cheap in comparison to their value.

Now we all know that when we look at an object, the image of that object is transferred through our eye-lens to the back of the eye upside down and to an area called the retina. The retina has three layers:

- The first layer has the **photo receptor cells** known as rods & cones. They are called as such because that's exactly how they look under the microscope and they help us distinguish light, color, shape, and distance.
- The second layer has the **bi-polar cells**. The bi-polar cells act as a medium to the third layer that makes a big difference in our lives.
- The third layer has the **ganglion cells** and these make the connection and bring in sensory data to your brain through the optic nerves. Believe it or not, it is your ganglion cells that decide what to draw to your attention and what to ignore during the day. But how do ganglion cells make these decisions?

Normally, unless something is *relevant* to us, in one way or the other, we will not really pay attention to it. Since the conscious mind can't handle everything we see for all of the obvious reasons we talked about earlier, it focuses on what is relevant and important to us and it deletes everything else the minute it labels it as irrelevant. In general, is what's relevant to a lawyer the same as to a surgeon, for example? Is what's relevant to a successful person the same as to an unsuccessful person? Is what's relevant to you the same as what's relevant to your brother or sister? You may have the temptation to say "Yes" but in reality the answer is "No". We all have a few things in common but not most important things in life are common to all people. If what's important to a successful person is also important to an unsuccessful person, the unsuccessful person would be as successful. If what's important to you, in general, is important to your neighbour as well, you'd have similar tastes in food, clothing, cars, sports, and so on. Do you? I doubt it!

Let me give you an example to make it clearer. A few years ago there was a scandal that almost toppled the largest dairy company in the world. Do you know which company I am talking about? *"Parmalat"*! Are you familiar with this name? For some reason I got interested in the story and I followed up on it for a couple of weeks and then it disappeared from the news. Up until that time, if you asked me whether Parmalat existed in Canada or not I would've said, *"I don't think so!"* Guess what happened to me right after? Suddenly, I started seeing Parmalat trucks all over the place. Did they just start operating in Canada? No, I think they were in Canada since I first arrived to this country, if not before. I simply didn't see it because it was irrelevant to me prior to that event and as such my brain induced a scotoma to handle other things that seemed more important at that time.

In a shopping mall, for example, there are literally thousands of items on display. Do you pay attention to every single item in the mall? You can, but normally you don't! When we go to a mall we normally pay attention to a few people, stores, and items on display based on the relevancy factor. Our brain selects what to bring to our awareness based on what it perceives as interesting, unique, and important. What is interesting and important to you in a mall may or may not be as interesting to your spouse, fiancé, son or daughter. So be patient when you accompany them to the mall and this is just to be fair. I admit it. When it comes to shopping, I am the hit and run kind of guy. I just go straight to what I want, buy it, and hit the road again. Guess who doesn't share this policy with me? You guessed it! My *"Significant Other"*!

The point is, when you go somewhere with someone, do you *see* the same things as they do? The answer is "Yes", but you don't pay attention to it equally. Your unconscious mind registers everything that goes on around you. But if your conscious mind did not receive any alert messages from your RAS, you will not pay attention to any of it. Your RAS will either make you oblivious to things that it deems as irrelevant, or it will literally make you abruptly turn your head to see something you find interesting such as a beautiful...car, bike, or house, for example. You know!

The "Relevancy Factor" applies to everything in your life, and your success, or failure, mainly depends on what your RAS selects and brings to your attention.

So what is the *"Relevancy Factor"* really telling us?

Two very important things:

1. It is telling us that if we're only interested in things that are counter productive to our growth, those will be the things that we'll see and pay attention to. Moreover, we'll become unaware of all the things that could help us succeed in life. That is to say, opportunities will be standing a few inches away from our noses yet we won't see them. Books and seminars that could change our lives will be all around us but we'll pass by them as if they don't exist. I bet you, the next time you go to the library or bookstore you're going to notice things that you've never noticed before. This is what the "Relevancy Factor" is all about.

We *attract* into our lives whatever is relevant to us and consider as important.

Accordingly, can you think of the many things that could've changed your life but you didn't pay attention to in the past? The more you think of it, the more careful you'll be with what to focus on from this moment on.

2. It is also telling us that our brains are *"Goal-Oriented"* and unless we consciously tell them what exactly we want, and what to look for, they'll wander and fill the void with counter productive thoughts we instilled in it throughout the years. That is to say, you have to know exactly what you want, to *see* what you want. The brain will not work on vague desires. It will only work on what you consciously and incessantly feed it, good or bad, positive or negative.

The whole point is, unless success, growth, happiness, and good health become sincerely relevant to you, and unless you develop a plan to achieve what you want in life, you won't be able to see all of the relevant things related to these issues even if they stand in front of you and call you by name. Conversely, when success, growth, financial independence, good health, and happiness do really become important to you, you will start noticing things that you've never paid attention to before. It's just how our brains work and now you know!

In summary then, it all starts with every conscious *thought* you choose to think of and how you utilize your *time* and *energy* to transform these thoughts into reality. Your life is the by-product of what you pay attention to and how your brain consolidates its energy toward materializing what's pertinent to you. It's about training your brain to automatically trigger successful *habits* that will enhance and stabilize your performance and help you move faster toward achieving higher goals. Added, your *reality* will always be based on what is *relevant* to you, and what you make it so will show up in your life.

Finally, I sincerely hope that the information you went through so far is more than enough to convince you that YOU ALREADY HAVE WHAT IT TAKES to become what you wish and really deserve to be.

Please proceed to Part Two to further learn about how to strengthen your success and get your life under control for as long as you live!

Part Two.

Your Success Recipe

Introduction

Welcome to Part Two. In Part One we talked about the ingredients of success: Our brain, how it really works, "why" we are what we are right now, and how our thoughts directly affect our health, mood, attitude, decisions, performance, outcomes, as well as our destiny. Nonetheless, we talked about the unlimited/true potential of our brain, how it normally brings to life whatever we focus on most of the time, and how it may deliberately induce a scotoma that will make us oblivious to opportunities available to us everyday.

In Part Two, we're going to talk about how to streamline your mind, heart, body, and soul, and put all of these in unison because this is the real secret to good health, wealth, and happiness. As has been demonstrated throughout the book, success occurs as the result of many factors that work together as one whole system rather than just focusing on one thing at a time. In this part we'll work further on ourselves, from the inside out, simply because unless we really change the inside, nothing significant will happen on the outside.

Part Two is mainly divided into three segments:

1. **The Clean-Up Segment** (*Chapters 10-13*)

2. **The Tune-Up Segment** (*Chapters 14-17*)

3. The Re-programming Segment (*Chapters 18-22*)

Each of these segments has three to four ingredients. Like any recipe though, you have to include all of these ingredients and apply them simultaneously. If you do that you'll notice drastic changes in your life within a short period of time and this will eventually bring about profound change in most aspects of your life.

None of these ingredients is hard to apply, unless you say so, and you'll be able to integrate each into your daily routine the minute you hear it. Some ingredients may take more time to sink in and become a habit. That is okay. Just be persistent and patient. Things will change!

The first ingredient, however, is the key that will open the door to your new life and to all of the other ingredients in this recipe. Unless you apply it, little will happen in your life. You might be surprised when you hear what the first ingredient is all about and I urge you to remain open minded until it has been explained. Are you ready? Ok, let's go to the next chapter.

Chapter 10

You Must *RYME*

"At this time and age if you're not entirely committed to success then you are automatically committed to failure"
–Saleem Bidaoui

The first and most important step to success, in my opinion, and which is based on my own experience, is to RYME. You might say, "What the heck is he talking about?" He's been okay until now. Well, please hold your horses for a minute! I just hope you did not get mixed up between RYME and Rhyme. It's not the *"Prime time kind of rhyme"* that I am talking about in here. R.Y.M.E. stands for: **R**emove **Y**our **M**ental **E**armuffs. Mental earmuffs are the seed of ignorance, prejudice, mediocrity and stagnation, to say the least. By keeping your mental earmuffs "ON", you literally create the scotoma, or blind spot, we talked about earlier.

I consider it as the first and most important key because until you RYME, nothing will happen in your life. Guaranteed! It took me so many years to figure that out. I spent over half of my life with my mental earmuffs "on", just listening to myself and no one else! It was only when I decided to remove my mental earmuffs that my whole world changed and I urge you to do the same.

Mental earmuffs create an invisible bubble that will influence your perception of the environment around you. It will make you think that you don't need any input from anything that's outside of you. You think you know it all, but in reality you may have little, or none, of what you need to succeed and until you open up, it will not happen. How do you know whether your mental earmuffs are on/off? Here is how:

- When people around you try to draw to your attention, in one way or the other, that you are not on the right track yet you are not receptive to their input and advice, you know that you have your mental earmuffs "ON".

- Any time someone talks to you and you just nod but with no intention to even consider what they are saying, you know that you have them "ON".

- Any time you give a Yes/But response, you know that you have your mental earmuffs "ON" because when you first say, "Yes" with "But" to follow, all you're saying is, *"I don't really care about your opinion. I just want to prove my point of view and win the argument"*, which means you're not listening.

- If this book did not benefit you in any way so far, then most likely it is because you have your mental earmuffs "ON".

- When you gladly consider any kind of criticism as it *may* be good for you, on the other hand, you know that your mental earmuffs are "OFF", your mind is wide open, and ready for input.

- When someone gives you advice and you say to yourself, *"What if they're right?"* you know that your mental earmuffs are "OFF".

- Any time you're willing to take responsibility for your actions, and willing to learn from your mistakes, you know that you have them "OFF".

Can you see the difference between the two mindsets? Removing your mental earmuffs, however, doesn't mean that you must accept everything you hear or read about. It only means that you moved yourself from a "Hard to *accept*" state of mind to an "Easy to *understand*" state of mind. Notice that I did not say "easy to *accept*" state of mind. Rather, I said, "easy to *understand*" mindset. That is, to become more open, receptive, and at least consider the advice provided before you reach a conclusion. When you do that, it stays in your mind as a reference and future option.

There were times when I considered something then forgot about it and then it flashed in my mind a couple of years after I heard it. The point is, at least it was there and my brain brought it to my attention at a time when I needed it most. The opposite is also true. The minute you decide that something is irrelevant to you, what do you think your brain will do? It will automatically delete it, right? Will your brain ever consider it again? Maybe, but most likely it won't.

All said and done, when someone's mental earmuffs are "ON", nothing we talked about all along would matter and most of the gems laid out in this book would mean nothing to them. That's why I consider it the first and most important step to your success.

Bottom line:

RYME and the world will *rhyme* with you.

Guaranteed!

The Serenity Prayer:

"Grant me the serenity to accept the things I cannot change, the courage to change the things I can, and the wisdom to know the difference"

– Reinhold Niebuhr

Chapter 11

Just Let Go

*"The heart has two pressure release valves, they are called:
Forgive & Forget"* –Saleem Bidaoui

Do you know how they capture monkeys in some parts of India? They bring a box that is made from bamboo sticks and it is open from one side. Right in the middle of that box there are also bamboo sticks with a very narrow gap between them and the monkey can barely fit its hand in there. Behind that narrow gap there is a banana hanging right in the middle of the closed portion of the box. When a monkey comes along and sees the banana it goes inside the box and slides its hand through the narrow gap and grabs the banana but can't take it out because the bamboo sticks are too tight. Since the banana is too important for the monkey, it doesn't let go and it stays in that position for hours until the trappers come back and close the box with the monkey inside. Forgiveness follows the same rule.

When I tell people they must *learn* to "let go", their first reaction is normally something like, *"But it's hard"* or, *"I can never do that!"* With such a response all they are saying is they want to keep on holding to their mental bananas. Yes, it is hard to let go sometimes. I said the same thing in the past then slowly taught myself to apply it and I urge you to do the same because it feels good.

Here's another secret to a better life:

The minute you learn to "let go" at will, you know that you are in control of your life rather than life controlling you.

But "let go" of what, you may wonder? The first and most important thing you can do to be happy and successful is to "let go" of your past. Forgive *yourself*, that is. Understand that mistakes are unavoidable and we'll keep on making them for as long as we live. That's human nature and that's how we learn to get better. I agree that some mistakes are bigger and more damaging than others. But what's done is done and we cannot go back in time to change anything. That is to say, you can't rewind your past and go back in time, not even for one second, to fix something that has been done by you, or unto you. It cannot be done and it will not help you at all to stick to that rotten or ugly banana for the rest of your life.

To insist on holding to bad memories and feel guilty about them has a negative impact on you. It directly affects your health, mood, decisions, sleeping patterns, your relationships, and you'll gain nothing in return.

Your best bet is to learn from your past and present mistakes and then automatically throw them behind you. By doing this you'll feel as if a mountain has been lifted off your back. Remember that feeling guilty about what happened will not fix any problem. It will only create more problems by making you live your life with this feeling of guilt. Trust me. I've been there and I have a huge inventory of mistakes! I was deeply hurt by some people and I've done some harm to others in the past. Worst of all, some of those whom I caused harm are no longer with us. Regrettably, I cannot go back and delete or fix what I've done. Yesterday is gone forever. I can only be good, and do good, today and tomorrow. This is my solace. The best you can do to have a better future is to let go of your past and forgive yourself. To do this is an opportunity to start all over again, and in a way that you really want. What a feeling indeed! To let go is another major step toward self-recovery and a fresh start in life…if that's what you're looking for.

Next, learn to forgive people who caused you harm, mentally or physically. Yes, some of us have scars so deep and find it extremely hard to heal and recover. But think about it. Who's the only person in pain because of ruminating on these memories? You, right?

By doing this can you change what happened? Of course, not! You cannot change your past and your best option for a brighter future is to *"Forgive & Forget"*. It may not be easy in the beginning, or you may not feel comfortable in doing so, but it is very healthy even to try.

Yes, you might be able to forgive. But how can you forget, you might say? I agree with you that you cannot delete what happened from your memory, but you still can change your focus and forget about it any time the bananas try to creep into your consciousness. By *"Forgive & Forget"* I mean to forgive forever and forget about it any time it shows up in your awareness. Now you know how to do that. Just change your focus and you'll snap out of it in seconds. Try it and you'll find it much healthier for your mind, heart, body, and soul. More than anything, it makes your life much less stressful.

Last but not least, ask the Creator to forgive you! This will help you to let go of your burdens and put your soul on the right track of life. Try it!

"Learn to live,
and live to learn"
-Bayard Taylor

Chapter 12

Stop Lying
To Yourself

"To survive is a given, to thrive is a choice"
–Saleem Bidaoui

"Fake it until you make it". Did you ever read or hear about such a misleading statement? Well, with all due respect to those who believe in doing so, I think that's an awfully wrong statement. The truth is that some of us have been faking it all of their lives and that's why they couldn't achieve anything significant so far. Now think about it. If you are fully equipped to succeed yet behave in a self-destructive way, would you be behaving naturally, or would you be faking it? I am sure you'll agree with me that if we already have what it takes to win the game of life yet behave otherwise, we would be faking it, right?

Training yourself to be good at something is by no means *"faking it until you make it"*. It's about slowly, but surely, developing the habits of success that we talked about earlier. *"Fake it until you make it"* teaches self-defeating hypocrisy and creates some confusion in the brain by teaching it to accept something contrary to the beliefs of a moral society. Whether you go to a church, mosque, or synagogue, we've all been brought up and preached to be true to ourselves and to resent faking it, or being fake. Unfortunately, nowadays some authors, trainers, and mentors, passively preach this slogan as a means to success.

The truth is, when you try to fake it you would be acknowledging and pretending that you don't have the right tools to succeed. In reality though, you are physically and mentally a healthy, well-equipped, ready, and capable being and perhaps all you need is the training, not the faking.

As discussed throughout the book, and as confirmed by neuro-scientists, we are very well prepared to succeed in every aspect of our lives; nonetheless, capable of achieving anything we can dream of and in most cases all we need to get there is to *"Stop Lying to Ourselves"*. We need to stop pretending that we can't get to that level where we deserve to be. The reality is, we don't need to fake it. What we really need is to be honest with ourselves about our *"True Potential"*, and who we really are. We need to stop faking that we don't have what it takes to succeed or be more successful beyond what we are right now.

As mentioned earlier, you can only achieve what you believe. If you believe that you can't, then you will not, and you would be lying to yourself, to your loved ones, and to everyone around you. Said differently, if you are mentally able and you believe that what you are not, you would be faking it. Here is an undisputed scientifically proven fact:

If someone else can do it, you can do it too!

Always repeat this to yourself:

If they can, then I can!

You are never given a dream without being given the power to achieve it, and if you fully understood what I said all along in this book, then you have the proof that you can. This is a scientific fact, not a claim, nor a mere fantasy. However, if I am not a living proof to this fact, then who is? Did I transform my self because I believed that I could, or because I kept on repeating to myself that I can't? If you still doubt yourself and what you are really capable of becoming, then please stop lying to yourself and stop faking it by saying that you don't have what it takes or you just can't do it. I assure you that you can be whomever, and whatever, you wish to be. All you have to say and repeat to yourself all day long:

Yes I Can!

Yes I Can!

Yes I Can!

*"It is in your moments
of decisions that your
destiny is shaped"*
–Anthony Robbins

Chapter 13

Avoid People
With PADS

"Life is a mirror of our thoughts"
–Saleem Bidaoui

Some people have what I call, "**Positive Attitude Deficiency Syndrome**", or PADS for short. Numerous studies have shown that people with PADS are highly contagious, draining to your energy, and damaging to your health because they create stress in your life, bring you anxiety, and weaken your immune system, to say the least. Having said that, then it's to your utmost advantage to stay away from such people or they'll easily suck you into their whirlpool of misery and ruin your life in the process. The next time you spend some time with such people just notice how you'll lack positive energy, enthusiasm, and motivation, during, and right after being around them. Such people radiate negative feelings to anyone that comes near them, or in contact with them. They just can't help it! But guess what? You can!

Stick around positive people, on the other hand, and they will boost your energy, make you feel good all day long, and they will give you unconditional support when-ever you need it. Moreover, research shows that positive people will literally boost your serotonin levels, which is the pleasure hormone, and will bring a smile to your face even if you don't feel like it. Do you see the difference between these two types? It is to your greatest advantage that you make the right choice.

A few years ago Anthony Robbins and Mark Victor Hansen, the co-author of Chicken Soup series, were guest-speakers at a convention. At dinnertime all the speakers were together enjoying each other's wit and wisdom. Mark joined Tony at his table and during the course of the meal he asked, *"Tony, last year you made $156,000,000 in training and public speaking engagements while I only averaged $1,000,000. How did you do that?"* Tony smiled and asked Mark, *"Who are the people in your Master-Mind group?"* Mark was quick to say, *"They're all millionaires".* Tony replied, *"Well, that's why! I sit with billionaires".* Yes, you may not be interested to go that far, and that's your choice. Emphatically speaking though:

We are what we think about…and whom we associate with.

In his book, *"The Success Principles"*, here is what Jack Canfield had to say about associating with positive people:

"Make a conscious effort to surround yourself with positive, nourishing and uplifting people – people who believe in you, encourage you to go after your dreams and applaud your victories."

It is wise to carefully choose the people you associate with as they are of great importance to your health, wealth, happiness, and success. Nonetheless, always visualize positive thoughts, places, and events. This will also affect every cell in your body, as well as everyone you come in contact with. Give what you need and it will come back to you in many folds and will make you feel good!

Bottom line: Avoid people with PADS and be positively contagious and you'll notice a positive change in your life.

Chapter 14

Welcome Your
Dis-comfort Zone

"Your fear sets your limitations"
–Saleem Bidaoui

Earlier we talked about the limbic system and said that, among other things, it is the emotional part of the brain. I also mentioned that the amygdala is the distribution center of our emotions. One of the amygdala's functions, however, is to induce the feeling of discomfort when we are exposed to a new task, or environment, because it wants us to stay within our *"Comfort Zone"* to keep us safe. The amygdala is always concerned about our safety. In the world we live in today this is somewhat counter-productive because if we follow our amygdala's instructions all the time, we'll never attempt to learn anything, or try to go beyond our comfort zone.

We all have fears, yet one of the most important differences between successful and unsuccessful people is how each deal with their fears when they arise. To unsuccessful people they are immobilizing. Successful people, on the other hand, face their fears by doing what they fear over and over again until those fears subside. I was thirty six years old when I attended college. It was then that I was introduced to public speaking and had been asked to speak in front of a group for the first time in my life. It was only in front of my classmates, but what a weird and uncomfortable experience it was. We were asked just to speak for two minutes each. When it was my turn, I felt pressure in my head due to excessive diversion of blood to my brain and felt that words were racing at 400 miles/hr. Everything around me was moving so fast that I honestly didn't know what I was saying. The whole experience lasted two very long minutes that seemed like hours. What caused all of my discomfort? It was my amygdala sending me signals that I was facing something new and uncommon.

A couple of years ago I went to Canada's Wonderland for the first time. Frankly, I was terrified to go on most of the rides in there because I've never done it before. Knowing what I know today about stretching my comfort zone, I decided to go on a collision course with my fears. I decided to conquer my fears by going on the kids' roller coaster as a first step (*Yeah, you can laugh*). A couple of weeks after I tried something more challenging, but still moderate, and kept at it until I felt comfortable with it. Week after week, I kept on challenging my fears and upgrading from one ride to another until I became obsessed with these rides and felt like a kid again. A few weeks later I went on the most exhilarating (or terrifying) rides in the park and loved every second of it. Did you notice how I used the word "exhilarating" instead of terrifying? Was it scary in the beginning? You bet it was! But trust me, when you decide to go on a collision course with your worst fears, "You" will conquer "Yourself", your fears, as well as your most inhibiting habits, and what a feeling indeed. It's a feeling of total control, confidence, and power.

Learn to conquer and steer your fears and you'll accomplish another milestone toward your success and happiness. You don't have to do something dangerous to prove yourself. You don't have to go bungee jumping, or on a roller coaster, if you don't want to, but you still have to learn how to face and control your fears... that's if you are sincere about your success and happiness.

Let me tell you another story. In 1997, I was offered a job that changed the entire course of my life. I accepted a respectable position with an American training company as the Regional Sales Director for the whole Middle East. My job was to select and train salespeople to sell our company's training programs to organizations in the region.

Frankly, that's where I got hooked to training and that's where I stumbled on what I really love to do for the rest of my life. But as they say, there's no such thing as a free lunch, and good things don't come easy.

One day the CEO asked me to conduct an introductory presentation about the benefits of our training programs. As such, we invited managers from different companies to attend this presentation and approximately twenty-five managers showed up. At show time I came in, greeted the audience, and then just froze. My brain shifted to neutral and went completely blank. My heart rate went up to 500 beats per minute and I felt that my head was heavy due to the overflow of blood rushing in. Honestly, right at that moment I wished that the floor would open up and swallow me. That's how embarrassed I was. Can you imagine what happened afterwards? Well, I lost respect at work and my job was to follow. Did I bounce back from what seemed as a permanent injury? Yes I did! I refused to succumb to defeat. How did I do it? Well, with regard to public speaking, I became suicidal. That's how. I decided to do it and keep on doing it regardless of the consequences. So guess what I did right after that incident? I started a sales training company. Crazy, isn't it? The reality was, I decided to go against all odds and conquer my fears at any cost. Nowadays, I still have butterflies in my stomach when I speak in public but I learned to cope with those fears rather than letting my amygdala steer my behaviour to embarrassment. Now I feel that public speaking is somewhat within my comfort zone and I handle it by opening my speech with something nice and easy to say and then wait for my amygdala's attack to subside and I start having fun right after. What did this do to my comfort zone as a result? It expanded it!

So from now on, anytime your amygdala induces discomfort

to make you feel uncomfortable and edgy, just do it anyway. Nonetheless, say "Thank you" to your amygdala because this feeling is a message that you are about to sustain growth and you are on the right track to success.

Another way to expand your comfort zone is to embrace your mistakes...when they occur. As I told you earlier, the year 1999 was the worst year of my life. While we were still in the middle of that fiasco, my wife came to me one day trying to console me and make me feel better. She said, "Look what they've done to you". I looked at her and said, "We came here with our own feet. Nobody forced us to be here". Honestly, for the first time ever, I felt that I was in control of my life. For the first time in my life, I felt that I had learned a very good lesson. I accepted my mistakes and took the blame for what happened to my family and me. For the first time I refused to point fingers at anyone and felt so great about it.

Putting the blame on others will only tell your brain that it is not your problem and you don't have to deal with it, or even try to correct it. What happens as a result? Your *"Failure Mechanism"* is deactivated, you'll remain bound by the same mistake, and you'll do it again, as a result. Will this expand your comfort zone? No, it will not! Thus, learn to embrace your mistakes because you'll sustain growth, feel better, and you'll become much more confident.

Chapter 15

Balance Your Diet

"The problem is not when we eat to live, the problem is when we live to eat" –Saleem Bidaoui

If you have an expensive sports car and you always fill it with low octane gas, how will it perform? Like a clunker, right? Well, if that exquisite car is your own body and you use bad fuel everyday, will it perform perfectly well on the tracks of life? No, it will not! Why? Because food is the only fuel our body uses to sustain life and, as such, it has a direct impact on our health, decisions, mood, performance, relationships, as well as our intelligence. That is to say, food is fundamental to our brain's electro-chemical patterns and affects everything we do.

Therefore, if you strive for balance and better performance, be it mentally or physically, what shall you do? Have a balanced diet, right? Does it mean that you have to follow a strict diet? Well, I am neither a doctor, nor a nutritionist, to advise you on what you should or should not eat and before you decide to change your diet I strongly recommend that you consult your doctor.

Why a "balanced" diet? Simply because:

Our quality of life is largely dependent on the quality of food we consume everyday.

Three Fundamental Questions

Here are three questions pertaining to your health, happiness, performance, and success:

1. *Is it okay to skip a meal?* (Explained earlier)
2. *Does what I eat, and the time I eat it, affect my energy and sleeping patterns?*
3. *If I have an important meeting and need to be alert and full of energy, do I know what to eat, or not to eat, before that meeting?*

These issues are directly related to food and affect every aspect of our lives. Thus, it's imperative to know not only what kind of foods to ingest, but also when to do it. Using the right fuel at the wrong time is as damaging as eating the wrong food at any time. When and what to eat should be significant to you because it is eating the right food at the right time that creates balance within your brain, body, and life.

Food Structure

To understand how food affects our lives, let's briefly go over its structure first, and then discuss some guidelines that will drastically enhance your mental as well as your physical performance.

As we all know, our food is mainly divided into three categories:

1. **Carbohydrates**

2. **Protein**

3. **Fat**

1. **Carbohydrates**

   Carbohydrates are the main source of energy to the human body. They are divided into two types, depending on how fast or slow they are digested and absorbed by the body:

   a) **Simple Carbohydrates**

   Simple carbohydrates are easily digested and quickly converted into blood-sugar starting in the mouth. They give us a quick boost of energy and then a crash-landing right afterwards. Thus, they ought to be kept at a minimum per day and avoided as much as possible. They are mainly found in fruits, milk, white bread, white sugar, processed and refined food. Sugar and white-flour, in specific, have an adversarial effect on our overall health and they dull the brain, to say the least. They won't make us stupid, but research shows that they'll negatively affect our intelligence when we consume them.

   b) **Complex Carbohydrates**

   Complex carbohydrates, known as starches, take longer for the body to digest and thus make a better solution for steady energy. They're found in vegetables, products made of whole grain, brown rice, and legumes. Complex carbohydrates foods are said to allow more of the amino-acid *"Tryptophan"* to reach the brain resulting in a calming effect. Tryptophan, called by some *"The natural Prozac"*, is said to be a precursor to serotonin leading to a sense of satiety, relaxation, and feeling of pleasure.

2. **Protein**

   Protein helps to build up and maintain body tissues. Added, it contains the amino-acid *"Tyrosine"* leading to alertness and stable memory. It is mainly found in meats, lentils, soy, eggs, and milk.

   Now having said that, if you have an important meeting right after lunch and you need to be alert, what do you order, chicken or pasta? Chicken, right? Even if your chicken order comes with bread and salad, for example, make sure you start with chicken because you want your taste buds to detect it first. That is, to send a message to your brain to release the right hormones that will keep you alert for that meeting.

3. Fat

Does our body need Fat? Yes it does, but in minute quantities. The general rule about fat is this: "Bad Fat" is our body's natural enemy. Notice that I said "Bad Fat" and that is because our brains are mainly made of fat and we don't want to get rid of this kind of fat, do we?

Keep in mind that one gram of carbohydrates or protein contains four calories each. One gram of fat, however, contains nine calories, which is twice as much of the other two. What do excessive calories convert to? To fat, right? What happens when our body converts excessive calories to fat? We'll get fat and then look for ways to burn it off. Therefore,

When it comes to fat: when you eat it, you wear it!

Eating & Drinking Guidelines

The following are general guidelines that I personally adhere to. Always remember, however, that what may be optimal for me may be harmful for you. Thus, whatever your choice may be, please consult with your doctor before you resort to any change in your diet.

1) Stick to Five Meals

That is, three major meals, and two light snacks in between. As mentioned earlier, skipping meals during the day will deprive you from replenishing your energy, make you feel drained, and will lower your intelligence at a time you really need it.

2) Only One Protein Meal

As a general rule, eat one protein meal per day and the rest make it from Complex Carbohydrates. This will bring equilibrium to your body and you'll sustain better health and energy as a result. Don't worry about fat consumption as it will take care of itself due to its presence in almost everything we eat these days. That is to say, our body needs fat but there is no need to go after fat per se.

3) **Stay Hydrated All Day Long**
   Depending on its purity, water has tremendous benefits to our body, and brain. Here are some characteristics of the water we drink every day:

   - *Lubricates the brain*
   - *Dilutes impurities*
   - *Improves health*
   - *Good for the skin*
   - *A natural diuretic*
   - *Calorie-free.*

   Almost 70% of our body is made of water and 94%of our blood is water. A fundamental question is this: *What kind of 70% do you have in your body?*

   Water purity is normally measured by TDS (*Total Dissolved Solids*) that it may contain. The higher the number of these solids, the more contaminated it is. When measured by a *"TDS Meter"*, tap water shows that it contains about 290 ppm (*parts per million*). I am appalled by the labels of bottled water sold in the market today. Most bottled water sold in the market contains between 290-520 ppm, which is equal to, or worst than tap water. People either buy bottled water because of its brand name, or simply because it tastes like tap water.

   Here's the rule:

   If it tastes like tap water, most likely it is!

   We are not only what we eat, but what we drink as well. Two types of water are the purest and highly recommended by health specialists and microbiologists:

   a) Distilled water, which is 100% pure water, and

   b) Filtered by a *"Reverse Osmosis"* system. This process

purifies 99% of the impurities found in water today.

Now, depending on your climate and your daily activity, you should drink enough water during the day to keep your body, and most importantly your brain, hydrated and lubricated. If you still remember, earlier I said that the gap between brain cells is filled with CSF (*Cerebral Spinal Fluid*), which is mainly made of water. That is to say,

The minute you feel thirsty, it means that your intelligence already dropped by an average of 20–30%.

Your brain does not have any sensory cells to inform you of this deprivation and decline, thus, you will not feel it until you really need it. So beware!

4) Limit Your Coffee Consumption

Coffee is an addictive drug that is used as a stimulant. It is diuretic and not a substitute for water. Which means, when you drink coffee your body will get rid of it without benefiting from the water part of it and this will dehydrate your body faster.

Coffee also produces a hormone that accelerates aging. Thus, drinking too much coffee during the day is like putting your aging-process on fast-forward, mainly your skin. How do you know you are addicted to coffee? If you experience any withdrawal symptoms, such as headaches, when you try to stop drinking coffee, then you know that you are addicted. It has been said that drinking up to two cups per day is okay for some people.

Drinking coffee at night, however, is the worst thing you can do to your body. It is a time when it is supposed to relax and switch gears to slower brain waves. What could be a good alternative in the evening? Drink a cup of milk instead, if you can! Milk contains the hormone melatonin which is naturally produced by your body to slow you down and eventually put you to sleep.

5) Eat Desserts At Night

If you can postpone eating desserts to just before bedtime, that would be great. Doing so will give you an initial spike of energy and then a crash right after. It will help you sleep faster, that is.

Final Advice

Certain foods have certain effects on certain people. Your body will give you the right prescription and response on what to eat, and when to eat it. Try to establish a "Food Portfolio" for what's best for you and the best time to eat each type of these foods. Immediately respond to your body's messages and you'll see substantial changes in your health, mood, and intelligence. You'll be more energetic, feel better, sleep better, and you'll be in a well balanced mood... most of the time.

Just remember this all time wisdom:

We are what we eat...and drink!

"Life will get better when you play it by the rules"

– John M. Templeton

Chapter 16

It Is Wise
To Exercise

"Life is an escalator and we choose its direction"
–Saleem Bidaoui

The word "exercise" comes from the Latin root meaning "to maintain, or to keep". Another ingredient that will help you maintain and improve your physical as well as your mental health is exercise.

Can exercise be a direct contributor to your success? Studies show that people who walk rapidly for 45 minutes, for at least three days a week, demonstrated a substantial improvement in their executive cognitive functions such as planning and working memory. Consequently, their brain-wave tests showed a 35-millisecond faster response time after the exercise in comparison to pre-exercise response.

Benefits of exercise

Here are some of the benefits of exercise that will directly contribute to your well-being, energy, mood, and everything else in your life:

- **Exercise Increases**
    - *Overall energy*
    - *Self-esteem and self-confidence*
    - *Mental focus*
    - *Strength and stamina*
    - *Bone strength*
    - *Muscular strength*
    - *Lean muscle tissue*
    - *Metabolic rate*
    - *Body density*
    - *Cardiac output*
    - *Heart size and weight*
    - *Reaction time*
    - *Range of motion*
    - *Ability to relax*
    - *Productivity*
- **Exercise Improves**
    - *Glucose regulation*
    - *Cardiovascular function*
    - *Your immune system*
    - *Psychological well-being*
    - *Digestion*
    - *Body shape*
    - *Endurance*
    - *Quality of sleep*
    - *Appetite for healthy foods*
    - *Body posture*
    - *Sexuality*
    - *Coordination and balance*
    - *Oxygen circulation*
    - *Flexibility*
    - *Liver function*
    - *Blood flow*
    - *Body use of calories*
    - *Weight control*
    - *Muscle chemistry*

- *Chances of living longer*
- *Self-image*
- *Skin tone and complexion*
- *Overall quality of life*

■ **Exercise Decreases**
- *Blood pressure*
- *Body fat*
- *Cholesterol level*
- *Risk of developing diabetes*
- *Risk of colon and breast cancer*
- *Arthritis symptoms*
- *Risk of osteoporosis*
- *Number of sick days*
- *Chance of premature death*
- *Risk of a heart attack*
- *Risk for heart disease*
- *Risk for stroke*
- *Symptoms of depression and anxiety*
- *Stress levels*
- *Joint discomfort*
- *Varicose veins*
- *Back problems and pain*
- *Frustration with daily problems*
- *Menstrual cramps*

Before You Start

I hope I gave you enough reasons to get you started. If you have been inactive for a while, however, you must start easy and slowly. The type, intensity, duration, and frequency of your exercise will depend on your physical condition. Never start a program without consulting your doctor first.

Here are few things you should be aware of before you do anything:

1. Choose an activity that you will enjoy.

2. Start at a slow pace and then proceed slowly.

3. Try to exercise in a group setting in the beginning.

4. Avoid any exercise that could hurt you.

5. Postpone your exercise in extreme hot or humid weather.

6. Avoid exercises that involve strenuous knee bends and vigorous turning of the head and neck.

7. Stop and immediately consult your doctor if you experience any of the following symptoms: *nausea, dizziness, shortness of breath, tightness in the chest, or persistent muscle soreness.*

Take-A-Walk

If you hate routine as much as I do, then maybe walking is the ideal exercise for you. Besides all of the benefits mentioned above walking has many extra benefits you can add to your list. Among these:

-   You don't need special equipment other than a comfortable pair of shoes…and a bottle of water.
-   You can do it anytime and anywhere, from your corridor to the beach, the park, or the mall.
-   You don't have to stick to a specific routine. It can be done in the morning, lunch-hour, or in the evening.
-   You can incorporate it with other activities.
-   Doesn't require too much effort.
-   There is no need to change your clothes.
-   Will clear your head and make you think better.
-   You can use it as a time for reflection.
-   You can do it with someone whom you enjoy a good conversation.

Whatever your preferences may be, exercising at least three to four times a week should be the norm. You stick to that and you'll notice a big difference in everything you do. Again, please consult your doctor and do a couple of tests to make sure you can handle it then start right after.

Have Fun!

Chapter 17

Sleep Well

"Sleeping deficit is malpractice"
–Saleem Bidaoui

Another major contributor to your success is to train yourself to sleep relatively early and well. It could be hard for you in the beginning but remember that most successful people sleep early and wake up early as well. This is not a coincidence, by the way!

We talked earlier about how the retinas have three layers and how the photoreceptors sense shapes, depth, distance, movement, and light or lack of it. These waves are transferred to a medium layer called the bi-polar layer then to the decision maker layer known as the ganglion cell and then to the brain through the optic nerves. The right eye's optic-nerves send information to the left side of the occipital lobe which is at the back of the brain and handles the sight functions, and the left eye's optic-nerves send information to the right side of the brain. Right at that intersection where information criss-cross from one side of the optic-nerves to the opposite side of the occipital lobe there is a cluster of specialized cells called Supra-Chiasmatic-Nuclei, or SCN, for short. The SCN's main job is to get information from the optic-nerves about light & darkness. Again, if anything, this also validates the significant role that our eyes play in our lives.

When the SCN senses darkness, for example, it stimulates the pineal gland to secrete the melatonin we talked about earlier which sends messages to our nervous system to make us feel sleepy and help us fall asleep. When it senses light, on the other hand, it sends messages to release cortisol into our blood stream to wake us up.

Okay, what does all of this mean? It means that if we work a night shift, sleep late at night, or do not have enough sleep, we are causing a hormonal imbalance in our body that will affect our health, mood, concentration, and everything we do during the day. All said and done, a good night sleep is another way to control your electro-chemical process and get the best out of it.

Here's what Ben Franklin had to say about this:

"Early to bed, early to rise, will make you healthy, wealthy, and wise".

Benefits of a Good Night Sleep

Other than the hormonal balance factor, which is central to a balanced life, there are further benefits. A good night sleep:

- *Rests body and brain*
- *Boost immune system*
- *Improves mood*
- *Reduces stress*
- *Replenishes energy*
- *Consolidates memory*
- *Discharge tensed emotions*
- *Help you look better*
- *Make you more alert*
- *Increases your concentration* (Major causes of work-related and car accidents are due to lack of focus and concentration)

Suggestions

In case you're wondering about the things that could help you to have a good night sleep.

Here are a few tips:

- *Avoid working nightshifts*
- *Avoid caffeine in the afternoons*
- *Avoid alcohol*
- *Avoid heavy meals in the evening*
- *Avoid smoking because it is a stimulant*
- *Avoid watching TV and violent shows in bed*
- *Avoid counting sheep to sleep* (It engages the brain)
- *Get sunlight during the day*
- *Take a nap after lunch, if you can*
- *Take-A-Walk after dinner*
- *Establish and stick to sleeping and waking up time*
- *Darken your room and avoid lights*
- *Maintain your ideal room temperature*
- *Get yourself a comfortable mattress and pillows*
- *Go to sleep only when you feel like it*
- *Drink a cup of milk or sedative herbs before going to bed*
- *Use relaxing and soothing aroma*
- *Relax your muscles and deliberately slowdown your brain activity.*

Good Night!

"The greatest obstacle to progress is not ignorance, but the illusion of knowledge" -Daniel J. Boorstin

Chapter 18

Destiny By Design

"In life, if you really don't know where you're going, that's exactly where you'll end up" –Saleem Bidaoui

Besides the fundamental reasons we talked about earlier, why should we set goals for ourselves? Here are four more profound reasons:

1. **Because life will not normally go according to plan if you don't have one!**
2. **Because if you don't stand for something, you'll fall for anything.**
3. **Because goals induce permanent self-motivation.**
4. **Because it tells your R.A.S. what exactly to look for and this will help you *see* it.**

Write Down Your Goals

Why should you write down your goals? The beauty and power of written goals lies in the fact that they harness our energy, mind, heart, and soul, toward the realization of our dreams. They'll *"show & tell"* the brain what exactly to look for, work on, and what to go after and achieve rather than just leaving it running on autopilot as most people do.

Hypothetically speaking, let's say I invited two people to Kuala Lumpur in Malaysia and when they arrived there I instructed both to meet me in Singapore the next day. However, I gave the first person a car, Malaysian money (*Ringgit*), and a detailed map of the region then gave the second person a car and Malaysian money but no map. Now, which one do you think will get to Singapore much faster? The first person, right? Why? Because he has a *clear map* that he can see and follow. As for the second person, he may or may not get to Singapore at all. It's all left to luck!

Well, our brains work in exactly the same way! When we provide them with a clear map of what we want they will create a clear picture of what exactly to work on and then will utilize their powerful resources to materialize what we want. Not only that, but will also feed that information to our RAS and consequently we'll become aware of the things and opportunities that will help us achieve our goals and make them real.

Your Blueprint to Success

Just like going from Kuala Lumpur to Singapore, the first step to reaching any destination is to find out where you are right now, what you have, and what you don't have. It is about taking count of your educational, financial, and emotional inventory. Are you currently a college graduate and need an MBA to fulfill your dreams? Do you have enough money to support yourself and your family for this trip? It's imperative to write down your starting point on paper so you won't forget where you started, and to monitor your progress. Some people forget their starting point and can't see or measure their progress because it is incremental, but not substantial, and they lose hope and enthusiasm along the way. I strongly advise you to start with your status quo before writing your goals.

The second step to getting what you want in life is to think of your destination clearly and in minute details. To decide where exactly you want to go, that is. "I want to be successful" is not a destination. It doesn't tell your brain what exactly to bring to life. "I want to be a successful ...*writer*", for example, is a destination.

The third step to achieving what you want is to draw a map and devise a plan on how to get there. How can you draw a map and feed it to your loyal servant? Clearly state your goals on a piece of paper. That is how!

The Process

Okay, you know exactly where you want to go and what you want to be in life. It's time to devise a systematic approach to how you're going to get there. There are three steps to draw your success blueprint:

1. Your Mission Statement

Just before defining and writing your goals you must clearly state your mission in life because it is at the core of your values and beliefs. It defines who you really are and what you love to be, or do, for the rest of your life.

Is your mission part of your goals? They are strongly related, but your mission is not a goal. Actually, there's a huge difference between the two. Your goals have a deadline and they become history the minute you achieve them. That is, once they are a reality, you forget about them and start looking for new ones to pursue. Your mission, on the other hand, once defined, it becomes a never-ending process and you keep at it for the rest of your life.

To give you a vivid example, here's my mission statement:

"My mission in life is to help people succeed and others to proceed"

Does my mission have a deadline? No, it doesn't! It is an incessant process that I can keep on doing and enjoying for as long as I live. Is this book part of my mission? Well, if you're reading it, then it is, I guess!

Having said that, start your goal setting process with the following questions:

• **What is my mission in life?**

How would you like to help and benefit the world that is? Is it by helping people live better, helping the blind, the homeless, the abused, or is it by keeping your city green? It boils down to your passion. Ask yourself:

• **What is my real passion in life?**

Write it down and visualize it on a regular basis. If you can't think of your mission right now, that's okay. You can proceed to defining your goals and then come back and define your mission.

One more thing about your mission. Do you still remember my definition of success?

Just in case you forgot it, here it is:

"Success is the realization of something you love to be or do for the rest of your life"

Now go back to the previous page and compare it with my mission statement. Do you see the correlation between the two? In essence, they are inseparable and mean the same thing.

2. Your Macro-Goals

A Macro-goal is the exact port you'd like to reach and dock at by the end of each significant journey in your life. It is the final destination for something you strive for. It defines what you really want and deserve to be, or have, in life. In other words, it is one of your Master-Goals in life. Micro-goals, on the other hand, are about *how* to get there. They describe the means to a desirable end.

Here are three macro-goals that you must answer before you proceed to your micro-goals:

■ **What would I love to do in life, even if I don't get paid for** it?

Here's how to handle this question: Name three things you would love to do in life and then narrow it down to your most desirable one among the three. The answer to this question will define your real passion. Spare the "*how*" for now. Just focus on what you love to do, not how you may or may not get there. Leave this task to your loyal servant.

- **What is that one thing I am willing to invest ten years of my life to achieve it?**
Is it a Masters Degree in something you love to do, or is it a research project that will benefit society and get you recognition? What is it that you don't mind sacrificing ten years of your life in order for you to have it? Here's the sad news about this issue, however:

If you say you cannot, you will not!

Do you still remember the elements of manifestation? They are *thought, time,* and *energy.* Whatever you want to see in your life, you must invest these elements in mastering it first, and there's no other way around it! Next:

- **What do I have to eliminate from my life in order for me to succeed?**
Is it ignorance, procrastination, smoking, extra weight, a few bad habits, or a relationship that is going nowhere? What is it that you can no longer afford to tolerate and it is adversely affecting your mood and energy?

Write down your macro-goals questions and answer them before you work on your micro-goals. Remember, by doing so you are directing your brain to work on what you want to recognize and see in your life. Your goals will activate your RAS, as well as your senses, to be on the look out for opportunities relevant to what you want to achieve. Don't be surprised when you start noticing things that you've never noticed before. It literally works like magic!

One caveat: Your *"Mission Statement"* and your *"Macro-Goals"* must be congruent with each other. If they're not, then you either have the wrong mission or the wrong macro-goals.

3. Micro-Goals

Micro-Goals are about the means that will help you achieve your Macro-Goals. They describe what you should do and how to do it. The following are a few questions that will help you execute your plan:

1. What do I need to have or do in order for me to achieve what I want?

By answering this question you lay-down your sub-goals that will show you how to get there. That is, do you need to attend a specific course, a certificate or diploma, $50,000, or a special piece of equipment? What is it that you need to achieve your Macro-goals, that is?

2. If I start to work on my micro-goals today, how long do I need to fulfill my dream?

Is it approximately three, five, or ten years? Write-down your estimate and it doesn't have to be accurate in the beginning. All of your micro-goals will be subject to continuous modification and nothing is carved in stone. How often should you modify your micro-goals? At least once a year!

3. What shall I do this year to get me closer to my macro-goals?

Write down your answers in point-form (a, b, c, d).

    a) Apply for my Masters Degree

    b) Work to save $5,000

    c) Create my website

d) Stop smoking

4. **Repeat question #3 for the year after, and so on, until you fill up your 3, 5, or 10-year plan.**

By doing this, you can envision your target, and how to hit it; nevertheless, you can measure your progress. Added, you'll also enjoy every moment of the trip because you'll be doing something you love to do, look forward to doing it, and it has a significant meaning to you. More than anything, this will ignite your desire and make you fire on all cylinders... long-term.

Don't be alarmed or discouraged if you get off-course now and then because you will! No pilot takes-off and flies from point "A" to point "B" in a straight line and life is no different. Pilots normally get off-course 90% of the time but they constantly take corrective action until they arrive at their destination. I was off target for about three years, yet here you are reading my book! The key point in here is to remain focused on your master-goals regardless of the many challenges, distractions, and detours you may encounter.

Now here's how your trip toward achieving your master-goals may look like in the beginning: You are downtown and seeking to find your way to the highway. You may experience heavy traffic, many traffic lights, and a few detours. For those who don't have a plan, or map, that's where they get lost in life and start going in all directions. As for you, and since you have your map in front of you, detours will not distract you from reaching your "master-goals highway". As soon as you hit that highway, trust me, you'll feel it in your bones and from that time on you'll accelerate full speed toward your destination.

Bon Voyage!

*If you go to work on your goals,
your goals will go to work on you.
If you go to work on your plan,
your plan will go to work on you.
Whatever good things we build
end up building us"* -Jim Rohn

Chapter 19

Dream It To Achieve It

"Your imagination weaves your reality, choose your dreams wittingly" –Saleem Bidaoui

An essential and highly effective aid to your written goals is to fantasize or daydream, not only about your *"Master Goals"*, but also about every significant task you intend to undertake and every skill you need to master.

Earlier, we talked about how the brain cannot distinguish between real and imagined experiences, how the unconscious mind treats every input as real, and how it will always say to your conscious mind, *"Yes Master and let me help you live it"*. Further, we talked about how if there is a conflict between our willpower and imagination, our imagination will invariably win the day.

We also talked about how willpower alone will not be enough to do the trick and that we need assistance from our imagination to make things happen. That is, we need to create the image of what we want to achieve, first, so our mind could work on bringing it to reality. This will create the right network in our brain, even before we attempt to do the task, and will make it much easier and faster for us to master it once we start doing it. That is to say, dreaming it will create a symbiotic relationship between our willpower and imagination and that will accelerate our progress to realization of what we're after, tremendously.

Success Simulation Session

Besides merely dreaming it, there is a scientifically proven technique that will help you achieve better results in less time. It is known as the "Visualization" technique and I prefer to call it a *"Success Simulation Session"* because that's what distinguishes it from visualization sessions that unsuccessful people inadvertently play to themselves all day long. This technique is vigorously used by highly successful people and athletes. When athletes say that winning is 90% mental, they are specifically talking about this technique.

In his classic book, "The Art of War" Sun Tzu said,

> *"Wars are won before they are fought."*

What does it really mean? If anything, it means that wars are structured and rehearsed in the mind way before being engaged in reality. It also means to make sure that you dream about what you want, not about what you don't want to happen in your life.

In his book, "The Secret Power Within", Chuck Norris said,

> *"Always remember that success begins inside of you, if you can't see it first, now one else ever will."*

Well, that's what this technique all about. It's about synthetically engraining success in our mind. It's about creating that "synthetic experience" we talked about earlier.

The Process

To conduct an effective *"Success Simulation Session"*, however, here are six steps to rewarding dreams:

1. Find a very quiet place with no interruptions. Turn-off or completely lower the volume on your phone and everything else that might interfere with your session,

2. Sit down and close your eyes,

3. Take a deep breath and let it out slowly at least three times in a row,

4. Gradually work on relaxing all of your body muscles starting from your top and all the way down to your toes. This will put your brain in Alpha state which is the most receptive and conducive to learning,

5. Once you become completely comfortable and relaxed, play a positive movie on the screen of your imagination. That's right, you structure a beautiful movie in your mind about achieving and living your dreams.

   See yourself succeeding in your endeavour, sitting in your new office, driving the car you want, and living where you've always wanted to live. Such a fantasy is free and it will cost you nothing other than a few minutes of your time every day yet the rewards are phenomenal.

   If you are a salesperson, for example, fantasize about a successful meeting with your prospect. Imagine how you easily establish rapport, win their trust, and close the deal. You won't believe the effect it will have on you after awhile.

   If there is a skill you would like to master, play a successful performance of that skill over and over again. This will accelerate your mastery of that skill by ten folds.

6. Spend ten to twenty minutes on each session and use your five senses as much as you can as if you are inside that movie, not just watching it. See, feel,touch, and smell

everything around you as if you are really in the middle of that experience. Since your brain will not distinguish between this synthetic experience and reality, it will store it as a true experience and will start working on making it real for you. Remember, this is exactly how you programmed yourself in the first place. Thus, it is by using the same technique that you override the bad ones.

Again, and for all of the reasons we talked about earlier, please do not expect that *"Dreaming It"* will work like a magic pill. It will not! Like habits, you have to persist and give it some time to consolidate and form a network in your mind. After awhile though, you'll start noticing the difference in your progress, as well as in your performance. So go ahead and dream your way to a prosperous and more gratifying life. It is free and you have absolutely nothing to lose and every-thing to gain.

Chapter 20

Transformation
By Affirmation

"You can never achieve different results in life by adhering to your normal patterns of thinking" –Saleem Bidaoui

We are fully equipped to succeed, yet some of us instil *"Negative Affirmations"* in our mind, such as "I am a loser", and then start faking our ability and performance. Nevertheless, we re-enforce those affirmations by saying to ourselves something like, "I told you I am no good!".

Did you ever hear people saying: *"I can never be on time!"* or *"I am always late!"* Well, guess what these are? If you said negative affirmations, then you are absolutely right! They are affirmations rehearsed and re-enforced every day. What happens to those who use such affirmations? They are always late due to this self-fulfilling prophecy.

Negative affirmations don't sneak up on us and come to reality overnight, however. We normally repeat them to ourselves many times until our subconscious mind labels them as important and will save them in memory as such. What happens next? This information is fed to our nervous system and we'll behave accordingly. That's why we sometimes behave in contrast to our own expectations, by the way!

To meet our expectations, rather than defeating them, all we have to do is to reverse this negative process and re-instil positive ones. How can we do that? By using *"Positive Affirmations"* instead and until we see and feel the difference.

Again, here's the undisputable rule and the beauty of our brains:

Whatever we learn, we can unlearn!

That is to say, whatever we don't like and find counter-productive to our success, we can get rid of it and replace it by embedding the opposite to what we've inadvertently implanted earlier.

But what are positive affirmations and how can we effectively embed them in our mind? Positive affirmations are one-line short sentences we write on a 3"x5" card, or in our planner, and we repeat them to ourselves several times a day to eventually override any *"Negative Beliefs"* we may have.

Positive Affirmations

Here are a few positive-affirmations you can repeat to yourself everyday:

- **Self-Actualization**
    - *I like myself*
    - *I believe in myself*
    - *I am serious about my goals*
    - *I work toward achieving my goals everyday*
    - *I am always happy and excited*
    - *I am a happy person*
    - *I radiate happiness*
    - *I am always on time*

- *I am always positive*
- *I am more intelligent everyday*
- *I respect myself*
- *I accept myself exactly as I am*
- *I am a grateful person*
- *I am a capable and worthy person*
- *I am more confident everyday*
- *I love and approve of myself*
- *I set goals and achieve them easily*
- *I am a successful leader*
- *I am empathic and persuasive*
- *I have an excellent memory with easy recall*
- *I love to learn*
- *I am a learning magnet*
- *My learning abilities increase everyday*
- *I easily soak learning material*
- *I accept life's challenges*
- *I work on improving myself everyday*
- *I am a winner and always think like one*
- *I am a forgiving person*
- *I forgive myself and others*
- *I take full responsibility for my life*
- *I am always cool, calm, and collected*
- *I am always in harmony with myself and others*
- *I am always motivated to achieve what I want*
- *I always talk positive to myself and to others*
- *I am a positive person*
- *I always think positive thoughts*
- *I am a fulfilled person*
- *I live with integrity*
- *I take daily action to achieve my goals*
- *I work on creating successful habits everyday*
- *I learn from my experience and the experience of others*

- **Success**
  - *I am a successful person*

- *I am worthy of success*
- *I always expect success*
- *I am more successful everyday*
- *I imagine everything about my success in advance*
- *I visualize my success everyday*
- *I am a winner*
- *I am serious about my success*
- *I always experience the flow of prosperity*
- *My internal success is unlimited*
- *I do whatever it takes to succeed*
- *I contribute to my own and other people's success*
- *I think successful thoughts all day long*
- *I have the power and ability to achieve the success that I want*
- *I live with passion for success and excellence*
- *I have total confidence in my ability to achieve whatever I want*
- *I am committed to success*
- *I project success in everything I do*
- *I breathe success*

Work

- *I enjoy what I do*
- *I work on improving my _____ everyday*
- *I always give the best in me*
- *I manage myself well in stressful situations*
- *I am decisive in making important decisions*
- *I am serious about my work*
- *I benefit myself and others*
- *I am always on time*
- *I use my time wisely and effectively*
- *I am always eager to benefit myself and others*
- *I perform at my optimum level everyday*

Finance

- *I am a prosperity magnet*
- *I deserve to be well-off*
- *I love to make money*
- *I love being wealthy*
- *I respect those who accumulate wealth*
- *I make, invest, and spend my money wisely*
- *I am grateful for all of the abundance around me*
- *I handle my money wisely*

- **Health**
- *I get better and better everyday and in every way*
- *My performance is getting better everyday*
- *I am full of energy everyday*
- *I am more energetic everyday*
- *I wake-up full of energy*
- *I now eat healthy food*
- *I sleep easily and well at night*
- *I feel healthy and strong each and everyday*
- *I take excellent care of my body*
- *I am grateful for my strong and healthy body*
- *I have all the energy that I need to succeed*
- *I wake up feeling energetic everyday*
- *I respect my body*
- *I always feel and look healthy*
- *My body heals easily*
- *I wake up full of energy and refreshed everyday*
- *I am in control of my health*
- *I am physically fit*
- *I easily maintain my ideal body weight*
- *I love and take good care of my body*

- **Love**
- *I easily express love*
- *I radiate love*
- *I attract loving and caring people into my life*
- *I am loved by my family and friends*

- *I project love to everyone I meet*
- *I easily attract loving relationships into my life*
- *Love comes to me easily and effortlessly*

All of the above affirmations are for your benefit. I do, however, recommend that you establish two lists:

1. A *"Master-List"* for all of the affirmations that apply to you and find useful.

2. An *"Application-List"* that includes no more than 5–7 of the most important affirmations you want to immediately work on. Add new affirmations to your list as you feel comfortable with the ones you already working on.

To Make Them Work

Some people, however, claim that affirmations don't work. This is absolutely true if they are not well structured for the unconscious mind to accept them. The following are five guidelines to make them effective:

1. **Must be positive.**
   As mentioned earlier, if you write an affirmation like, *"I don't want to be a lousy salesperson"*, for example, that will only command your brain to act on the negative aspect of the message rather than your positive intent. To make them effective, affirmations must be positive and written in terms of what you want.

2. **Must be written in "Present-tense".**
   An affirmation like, *"I will be a master-salesperson"*, for example, is in the future-tense. Thus does not command the brain to act NOW. If I hold my wedding band in my hand and say, *"I will drop this ring"*, *"I will drop this ring"*. What will happen? Nothing! Now if I say, *"I am dropping this ring"*, then it's a totally different story, isn't it? So from now on use, *"I am so and so"* rather than, *"I will do so and so"*. That's how you talk to yourself and re-enforce all of your

affirmations, be it the positive or negative ones.

3. **Must be repeated.**

The brain is fresh and most receptive to input first thing in the morning. So take advantage of this and repeat your affirmation to yourself when you wake up. Some people write down their affirmations on a sheet of paper and stick it to their washroom's mirror and repeat them while brushing their teeth or shaving, for example. Put that sheet of paper where you can see it and let it act as a reminder. In addition, repeat them several times during the day and then repeat them a few times last thing at night so your unconscious mind can work on them and enforce them while you're asleep. Your unconscious mind never sleeps, right?

They may seem awkward in the beginning if this is your first time to use affirmations. Just remember that you do that everyday anyway. It is just that now you'll start doing it consciously and in a few weeks you'll be doing it, unconsciously.

4. **Make them believable.**

When you find an affirmation unrealistic in the beginning, add "I am in the process of..." to make it believable and acceptable. Don't write "*I am making $100,000*" while you are nowhere near it. Write, "*I am in the process of improving my income*" instead. It is more realistic and believable.

5. **Live and dream your affirmations.**

When you say to yourself something like: "*I am a successful person*", for example, integrate your affirmation with the feeling and vision of success. Synthetically live your affirmation, that is. This is extremely important to the attainment of your goals. Do not just repeat your affirmations like a parrot. They won't work that way.

Arnold Schwarzenegger, for example, did not become the Governor of California by merely saying to himself, "*I am just a body-builder*", "*I am just a body-builder*", right? It's very possible to achieve similar results provided you use the same,

    a)   *Empowering Affirmations* as he did

    b)   The same *Intensity of Desire* as he did, and

    c)   Take *Massive Action* as he did

How long should you use positive affirmations? *Until* you start seeing results. It might take three weeks, three months, or maybe three years. Keep on repeating them to yourself until you feel the change. That's how you programmed yourself to become who you are today and that's how you can *re-program* yourself to become what you deserve to be in the future.

Chapter 21

Invest In
Your Brain

"Reading is becoming!"
–Saleem Bidaoui

The majority of human beings have an *average* IQ and some of the most successful people on earth belong to this category. That is to say, they weren't born as geniuses, yet became highly successful. If that's the case, then what is the distinction that is making a big difference in their lives?

The Nurture Factor

Another dissimilarity between successful people and unsuccessful people, or any two people in fact, is one profound element:

People are either *"Nurtured Average"*, *"Semi-nurtured Average"*, or *"Un-nurtured Average"*.

Think about it. What differentiates any two human beings? One of the most important elements that distinguishes any two human beings is the degree of *knowledge* each has. Compare a successful person to a less successful or to an unsuccessful one. What you'll find first, and above all, is that the successful person *knows* what the less successful or unsuccessful person doesn't know. Compare a professional to any other person. What do you think the main difference between them is? Is it intelligence? Maybe! But most likely it is the *"Nurture Factor"*. One is intellectually nurtured, and the other one is not.

> *"We all have the same size of container between our ears. It's how much we put in it and offer to the world that counts. How much is an empty container worth to the world?"* –Saleem Bidaoui

Most of us were given the opportunity to become something enviable in life and were given the opportunity to acquire education up to any level we may have chosen. Some take advantage of this opportunity, while others decline it due to many reasons such as immaturity, bad influence, parents' ignorance, lack of vision, or neglect.

Sometimes all it takes is one lousy teacher to de-motivate you and ruin your life, as in my case. I was an average student and doing okay in school until I had to attend summer school and unfortunately had a biased teacher that did a good job in making me not only hate school, but learning altogether as well. I was young, naïve, and vulnerable. He was the kind of teacher that ruined the lives of many students. Sadly, I fell for his trap and paid the ultimate price. It took me a while to figure out the magnitude of the damage that I sustained. Luckily, I bounced back and re-built the life that I wanted, not the life that somebody else wanted for me, good or bad. The point is, regardless of where you are right now, it's never too late to start moving in the right direction. In the direction of the bright and better future that you deserve, that is.

Some people, however, halt their learning process the day they graduate. Mind you, *"Done with education"* is no longer valid at this time and age. The world is moving so fast nowadays that perpetual pertinent knowledge is not an option but a prerequisite to our success. What we acquire in college or university may remain relevant for a while but not for too long anymore and we need to keep up or we'll become obsolete in no time.

The highest paid and most successful people in the world read an average of 2 hours per day. Conversely, the lowest paid people don't read at all! Now let me ask you this profound question: *Do most successful people read because they are the highest paid, or are they the highest paid because they read?* Obvious, isn't it?

Further, it's been said that if you visit one of the highest paid people you'll find that the biggest thing they have in their house is their library. What is the biggest thing you'll notice when you visit the lowest paid people? The mega size of their TV, and they brag about it, right?

The Road to Glory

How much can you add to your growth without any progress in knowledge? Nothing, right? It's been estimated that we think about 50,000 thoughts a day. Now if your tomorrow's 50,000 thoughts are the same as today's 50,000 thoughts, will you have anything different in your life? Absolutely not! Therefore, unless you find a way to add pertinent knowledge, you have no chance to grow, mentally or financially.

If you ask me where did I really graduate from I'd say, "TPL & 401 Universities". That is, the "Toronto Public Library and the 401-Highway". That's where I acquired most of what I am sharing with you in this book. I had the privilege to learn and upgrade my skills, *for free*, at a time I couldn't afford buying or investing in anything. I am very proud of taking this path; nonetheless, grateful to the public library for the treasures they make available to us.

The point is:

You can be anything you want to be, and maybe for free, if you're committed!

You see, some of us commute an average of 20-30,000Km/Year. That's an equivalent to approximately 400 hours per year. Even with half of that time, just imagine the amount of knowledge we can acquire during that *"Dead-Time"*! You'll be amazed by the difference that it could make in your life just by utilizing this time toward acquiring *"Pertinent Knowledge"*. Just remember that by reading books, attending seminars, listening to CDs, mp3s, and downloadable e-books, it will be impossible for you to go back to the same level of knowledge or intellect you were before you've done so.

Neurologically speaking though, nothing revitalizes your brain more than new knowledge. So please, please, please, invest in your brain! It will literally transfer you from darkness to light. Once you see and feel that light, you'll become addicted to its rays and want more of it everyday. You'll be addicted to the dose of motivation and energy it will provide as well. Trust me, there is no feeling like it because you'll experience tingling in your brain and transformation on the spot.

Is reading, for example, a form of affirmation? That is, if you keep on reading and listening to self-development material, will it eventually sink-in and positively affects your life? You bet it will! Why? Simply because of the perceived *"importance"* and *"spaced repetition"* factors, right?

Any way you put it, there's no substitute to acquiring more knowledge every day.

Books That Make a Difference

On the following page is a list of books, CDs, and authors that made a big difference in my life. With all due respect to every other author, this list could serve as your initial library.

Normally, these books have references to many other books. You can start with the books I recommend and then branch off to any area of your interest. My advice is to buy these books and CDs one at a time, read or listen to them one by one, then do it all over again, and then do it one more time (*This also applies to the Anatomy of Success book, of course*). Once they become part of your life, you will not believe the impact they will have on you.

> *"If you want to earn more, learn more. If you want to get more out of the world, you must put more into the world. For, after all, men will get no more out of life than they put into it."* –William J. H. Boetcker

My Top-20 List

1. *Awaken The Giant Within*   Anthony Robbins
2. *Personal Power II.*   Anthony Robbins
3. *The Strangest Secret*   Earl Nightingale
4. *Life's Greatest Lessons*   Hal Urban
5. *Choices That Change Lives*   Hal Urban
6. *Psycho-Cybernetics*   Maxwell Maltz
7. *Advanced Psycho-Cybernetics*   Paul Thomas
8. *Self Mastery*   Emile Coué
9. *What Makes You Tick*   Thomas Czerner
10. *Create Your Own Future*   Brian Tracy
11. *As A Man Thinketh*   James Allen
12. *The Magic Of Believing*   Claude Bristol
13. *Think & Grow Rich*   Napoleon Hill
14. *How To Win Friends*   Dale Carnegie
15. *It's Not Over Until You Win*   Les Brown
16. *The Weekend Seminar*   Jim Rohn
17. *Secrets Of The Millionaire Mind*   T. Harv. Eker
18. *Principles Of Success*   Jack Canfield
19. *Power Of Intention*   Wayne Dyer
20. *Eight Weeks To Optimum Health*   Andrew Weil

"It's not what you know in life that will take you where you want to go, it's only what you're willing to act upon that will ever let you live your dreams"

– Robert Schneck Sr.

Chapter 22

Listen To Your Heart

"Your sixth sense is much more than a mere pump, use it" –Saleem Bidaoui

If your brain, with all of its features and functions, is planet "Earth" within the solar system of your life, then your heart is the "Sun" of that system. Last but not least is the final ingredient of your success recipe and that is to *"Listen to Your Heart"*.

Has this ever happened to you when you decided to buy a car, TV, or a house, for example, and you had a feeling that there was something not right about that deal? Some people call it a *"Hunch"*, *"Intuition"*, or *"Gut feeling"*. Call it what you want. It is your heart trying to talk to you. Can your heart really communicate with you? Yes, of course it can! Your heart does have intelligence. Scientifically speaking, it is known as your *"Second Brain"*. It has about 150,000,000 neurons, can think on its own, and it controls a good number of hormones in your body. So, never under-estimate your heart's intelligence and influence on your decisions.

How does it communicate with you? There are many ways where the heart sends messages to your brain trying to alarm you about something that you may have overlooked, or don't know what to do about it. It can either make you feel at ease, or uncomfortable, about a certain situation. It can make you feel concerned about something at a time where your brain can't put your finger on it. You normally feel that something is not right but you don't know what it is. Did you ever have such an experience? This is your heart's intelligence in action and this is how your heart communicates with you.

The damage is done when you have such a feeling and you ignore it and then go ahead with the deal anyway due to intimidation, pressure, or negligence from your side. Nine out of ten times you'll fall flat on your face and you'll live to regret it. When you train yourself to listen to your heart, however, you'll save yourself from the risk of becoming a victim, which is the last thing you want to do while you are on your way to success. Thus, it is in your best interest to train yourself to listen to your heart. When you encounter feelings of discomfort, especially when you feel that there's something fishy about a certain deal, stick to your heart's alarm. Just say to the person whom you think is causing this feeling in the first place, *"No thanks I don't feel comfortable about it and need more time to think it over."* I've done it so many times and never felt remorseful after. In fact, I normally feel delighted after because, in most cases, I end up doing the right thing and that's what matters most. Doing so will not only spare you a couple of headaches that you could do without, but also will make you feel proud of yourself and will put you in control of your environment. You'll become the driver of your life rather than a mere passenger. "Listen To Your Heart" is an ancient wisdom that remains valid until today and will be valid until the end of time. Try it! It will seldom disappoint you.

The Last Word

Now we come to the end of our journey together. I sincerely hope that I did a good job in trying to show you that you are ready and superbly equipped to reach any goal you may desire. Moreover, I hope that what I've shared with you in this book can make a big difference in your life as much as it did to mine.

Finally, let me summarize the wisdom of what we talked about in one quote made by Mahatma Ghandi. He said,

"Keep my words positive, words become my behaviours.

Keep my behaviours positive, behaviours become my habits.

Keep my habits positive, habits become my values.

Keep my values positive, because values become my destiny"

Best Of Luck!

Order / Contact Information

The perfect gift for those you care about!

Do you know a family-member, a friend, a colleague, or a client who could benefit from reading the *"Anatomy Of Success"* book? Why don't you send them a copy?

To order more copies of this book, please go to:
www.anatomyofsuccess.ca

Bulk Purchases & Discounts:
bulkorders@anatomyofsuccess.ca

Feedback:
Share your experience with me. Send me your comments and how this book has touched your life:
comments@anatomyofsuccess.ca

Mailing Address:

2900 Warden Ave,
P.O. Box 92122
Toronto – Ontario
Canada – M1W 3Y8

BUY A SHARE OF THE FUTURE IN YOUR COMMUNITY

These certificates make great holiday, graduation and birthday gifts that can be personalized with the recipient's name. The cost of one S.H.A.R.E. or one square foot is $54.17. The personalized certificate is suitable for framing and will state the number of shares purchased and the amount of each share, as well as the recipient's name. The home that you participate in "building" will last for many years and will continue to grow in value.

Here is a sample SHARE certificate:

THIS CERTIFIES THAT
YOUR NAME HERE
HAS INVESTED IN A HOME FOR A DESERVING FAMILY

1985-2005
TWENTY YEARS OF BUILDING FUTURES IN OUR
COMMUNITY ONE HOME AT A TIME

1200 SQUARE FOOT HOUSE @ $65,000 = $54.17 PER SQUARE FOOT
This certificate represents a tax deductible donation. It has no cash value.

YES, I WOULD LIKE TO HELP!

I support the work that Habitat for Humanity does and I want to be part of the excitement! As a donor, I will receive periodic updates on your construction activities but, more importantly, I know my gift will help a family in our community realize the dream of homeownership. **I would like to SHARE in your efforts against substandard housing in my community!** *(Please print below)*

PLEASE SEND ME _____ SHARES at $54.17 EACH = $ $_____

In Honor Of: _____

Occasion: (Circle One) HOLIDAY   BIRTHDAY   ANNIVERSARY

     OTHER: _____

Address of Recipient: _____

Gift From: _____ *Donor Address:* _____

Donor Email: _____

I AM ENCLOSING A CHECK FOR $ $_____ PAYABLE TO HABITAT FOR HUMANITY OR PLEASE CHARGE MY VISA OR MASTERCARD *(CIRCLE ONE)*

Card Number _____ Expiration Date: _____

Name as it appears on Credit Card _____ Charge Amount $ _____

Signature _____

Billing Address _____

Telephone # Day _____ Eve _____

PLEASE NOTE: Your contribution is tax-deductible to the fullest extent allowed by law.
Habitat for Humanity • P.O. Box 1443 • Newport News, VA 23601 • 757-596-5553
www.HelpHabitatforHumanity.org